MW01092605

ETHICS ESSENTIALS

FOR BUSINESS

LEADERS

Brian T. Engelland
Professor of Marketing
The Catholic University of America

William D. Eshee, Jr.
Professor Emeritus of Business Law
Mississippi State University

SophiaOmni Press

ETHICS ESSENTIALS FOR BUSINESS LEADERS
by Brian T. Engelland
    William D. Eshee, Jr.

Copyright 2007, Brian T. Engelland and
William D. Eshee, Jr.

Published by:

SophiaOmni Press
www.sophiaomni.org

ISBN: 987-1466234765

Printed in the United States of America

DEDICATION

This book is dedicated to the next generation of business leaders. We pray that you will be champions of sound ethical practice not only in the organizations you lead but in your personal lives.

PREFACE

Business ethics can be defined as moral principles and standards that one uses to guide business behavior. Judging by the recent wave of publicized ethics scandals that have affected corporate America, and recognizing that many of the executives involved hold business degrees from well-respected universities, it would appear that business schools have not done as good a job as is needed with business ethics education. Indeed, a study of business students in 13 top programs found that only 22% of respondents believed their ethics preparation was adequate, while 19% believed they were not being prepared at all. Critics have suggested that ethics coverage in business programs is rarely taught throughout multiple courses in the curriculum; that honesty, truth and fairness are often missing from curricula; and that students learn to treat the conduct of business much as a video game where one must "bend the rules" to achieve success.

An Ethics Education Task Force convened by the Association to Advance Collegiate Schools of Business (AACSB), the largest business school accrediting body, recently issued guidelines for business ethics education. The report recommends that "...business schools must encourage students to develop a deep understanding of the myriad challenges surrounding corporate responsibility and corporate governance; provide them with tools for recognizing and responding to ethical issues, both personally and organizationally; and engage them at an individual level through analyses of both positive and negative examples of everyday conduct in business."

The report also recommends incorporating four broad themes in ethics education: (1) the responsibility of business in society; (2) ethical decision-making; (3) ethical leadership; and (4) corporate governance. Finally, the report recommends that ethics coverage be extended to multiple courses so that ethics in marketing are covered in marketing courses, ethics in management are covered in management courses, ethics in accounting are covered in accounting courses, etc. In that way, students can more readily integrate and apply good ethical practices to their chosen discipline. This book is designed as a supplementary reading text that can assist instructors in integrating ethics into their business courses. It provides a sound basis in the essentials of ethics, and allows flexibility so that instructors can add articles from news magazines and business periodicals to illustrate examples of ethical issues and conduct. The book is designed to address the key priorities outlined by the Ethics Education Task Force. It portrays a coherent presentation of business ethics that incorporates good business citizenship, along with corporate and individual honesty, fairness and trust. The perspective we adopt is that even though ethical decision- making may be difficult, there is a right way to make such decisions, and ultimately, there is a right answer that is discernable. The decision framework and guidance offered in this book will help future leaders achieve proficiency in ethical decision-making, and lay the groundwork for them to become ethical leaders in the organizations in which they work.

The authors of this book have considerable experience regarding the subject of business ethics. One author acquired first-hand knowledge as a result of his positions as a marketing executive and consultant, and has regularly covered business ethics as an integral part of his undergraduate and graduate-level marketing courses. The other author has regularly taught business ethics for 30 years as a key component of his business law courses. In addition to his teaching experience, the second author has served as a municipal judge where he has been called upon to judge cases involving ethical issues in business, among other cases.

AUTHOR BIOGRAPHIES

Brian T. Engelland (DBA, Southern Illinois University at Carbondale) is Professor of Marketing in the Department of Business and Economics at The Catholic University of America. Dr. Engelland has 20 years experience in corporate business with 14 as a marketing executive in the building materials industry. As an academic, he has authored 65 refereed publications in marketing-related outlets and has co-authored four books. In the classroom, he has taught various courses in marketing, management, statistics, international business and business strategy. Dr. Engelland is actively involved in leadership of the marketing discipline, and is past president of both the Society for Marketing Advances and the Marketing Management Association.

William D. "Denny" Eshee, Jr., Attorney at Law (JD, University of Mississippi) is Professor Emeritus of Business Law at Mississippi State University. Dr. Eshee has both taught at MSU and served as a Municipal Judge for the City of Starkville from 1976 to 2009. He has been admitted to the following Bar Associations: Mississippi, Federal, Alabama, U.S. Court of Military Appeals and The U.S. Supreme Court. He has previously authored or coauthored seven books on business law. Dr. Eshee served over 30 years as a Judge Advocate officer in the Mississippi Army National Guard. He served as the State Military Judge for the State of Mississippi and retired as a Brigadier General.

CONTENTS

1

Why Business Leaders Make Bad Decisions

During the first few years of the new millennium, the United States witnessed an unprecedented number of ethical missteps among American corporations. High profile executives have been tried and found guilty of ethical violations ranging from fraud (Jeffrey Skilling and Kenneth Lay, former CEO's of Enron), larceny and corruption (Dennis Kozlowski, former CEO of Tyco), conspiracy and making false filings (Bernie Ebbers, former CEO of WorldCom), and insider trading (Martha Stewart, CEO of Martha Stewart, Inc.). The list of firms implicated in ethical misdeeds includes such major corporations as Arthur Andersen, Boeing, Qwest, Health-South, and Adelphia Communications. In the past four years, the Justice Department has secured more than 1000 criminal convictions or guilty pleas, including cases against more than 200 chief executives, company presidents and chief financial officers.

These ethical breeches have caused shareholders to lose billions of dollars, corporations to go bankrupt, innocent employees to lose their jobs, and a trusting public to lose confidence in corporations and corporate leaders. The number and severity of recent ethical breakdowns suggests that we are not dealing with just a few "bad apples." Rather, ethical violations appear to be widespread at the highest levels of all types of organizations. Sadly, what we've seen in the newspaper may be only the "tip of the iceberg" since most ethical lapses in America's organizations, corporations and institutions never appear in the news media. Certainly the leaders of American companies should be able to do a lot better than this. Why is it that so many business leaders make bad decisions?

Reasons for Ethical Failures

Unfortunately, business leaders often make unethical decisions. Research suggests that the reasons for these lapses include (1)undeveloped personal ethical standards; (2) leaving own personal ethical standards at home; (3) insufficient input from colleagues; (4) yielding to time pressures to make an incomplete or sub-optimal decision; (5) failing to install and adhere to an ethical code of conduct; and (6) favoring one stakeholder group over others. In the following section, we'll discuss each of these reasons.

Undeveloped Personal Ethical Standards. Most people learn and internalize their sense of ethical behavior many years before they assume positions of organizational responsibility. As a result of parental influences, sibling relationships and early socialization, children learn a sense of fair play, truthfulness, and respect for others that becomes ingrained and lasting. Continued training in ethics through schooling, study, reading and personal development, helps to develop new understanding that supports good ethical behavior by the time that the adult assumes a leadership position. However, when the leader is under-prepared and lacking in ethical training, the result can be *ethical myopia,* an inability to recognize ethical issues that require attention. Ethical myopia results in poor recognition of ethical conflicts, poor decision-making ability, and poor decisions.

An executive we know once remarked, "I know business

ethics. I took a college class in it once." It turns out that he took an undergraduate business ethics course as a college student 20 years previously, and he incorrectly assumed that he still knew everything he needed to know to operate ethically. Later we found out that this executive was leading an organization that had intentionally and systematically over-billed key customers for an extended period of time. When confronted with the evidence of this fact, the executive admitted that he didn't recognize the over billing to be ethical misconduct, but rather, just incompetent book-keeping. Obviously, one course in business ethics taken long ago is insufficient to overcome ethical myopia. Leaders need to continue to study ethics, recognize how ethical standards apply in various situations they encounter, and grow in ethical decision-making ability throughout their careers.

Leaving Personal Ethical Standards at Home. There is a tendency for some to mistakenly view business ethics differently than personal ethics. They engage in *ethical muteness* by withholding their own good sense from input into business-related decisions. Unfortunately, ethical muteness occurs at all levels of a business organization. We know of a young industrial products sales representative from the Midwest who was transferred to the New York sales district. After each sales call, the new representative   took   meticulous notes about what was discussed and specifically wrote down what the client said so that she could take appropriate follow-up action with the home office. After developing what she thought was a good relationship with one buyer, she was surprised to hear that buyer make a statement about competitive pricing that was very different than what she had written in her notes from the previous meeting. She was sure of her notes, so she said, "I'm really disappointed that you lied to me! I thought we were friends."

In reply, the buyer said, "Oh, but I like you. I would never lie to you as a friend. However, lying in business is expected.

You should have known that I was speaking in a business context when I told you that information!" Unfortunately, many business leaders get caught up in the mistaken idea that business is a game that is played by a different set of rules than their good sense dictates. They suggest that somehow honesty, truth and fair play should be set aside when you are talking about business; that all is fair in love and war, and business is war! Consequently, some leaders tend to park their own personal ethical sense at home, thereby denying its input on business decisions and creating many more incidences where their conduct and decision-making results in ethical misdeeds.

Insufficient Input from Colleagues. It has often been said that it is lonely at the top of an organization. This is due to the fact that the person at the top bears the ultimate responsibility for all the important decisions made by the organization. Some leaders make the job lonelier than it need be when they exclude the input of those in their organization with expertise on the matter under consideration. Part of the function of a good leader is to be open to constructive input and criticism, and use this input to make better decisions. Unfortunately, some leaders employ an autocratic managerial style that discourages open communications with those who work at other levels of the organization. As businesses become more global in scope and complexity, the acquisition of information needed to make good ethical decisions assumes greater importance. The input of experts who can provide cross-cultural understanding and insights is vitally important. Without access to all the information that is available, no wonder leaders sometimes make the wrong decision.

Yielding to Time Pressures. Executives are decision-makers. That's their job. Their day is filled with deciding which are the priority issues demanding their attention, deciding how to arrange their schedule, deciding how an impending crisis can be averted, deciding who to see, or deciding what additional information is needed to make a good decision in a specific case. The typical executive makes over 300 business decisions each day – that's an average of one every two minutes. Consequently, executives try to prioritize so that they can devote additional time and mental energy on the most important problems the business faces; and they learn to take short-cuts on what they hope are the less important decisions. Executives may ignore a problem, rely on a subordinate to handle it, or make a gut-level decision without obtaining data. Just as a baseball player isn't expected to get a hit with every at bat, an executive realizes that not every decision will be a good one. There simply isn't enough time in the day to make a well-considered determination in every situation. This "bias toward action" is an admired trait, but it carries a potentially large downside.

Bernie Ebbers, the CEO and driving force behind the creation of WorldCom, used this defense at his trial. His company had overstated quarterly profits by $3.8 billion, which misled investors, and caused WorldCom stock to rise beyond its true market value. Mr. Ebbers maintained that the overstatement of earnings was not his fault; rather it was due to deceptions devised by the financial experts that he had hired and entrusted with managing and reporting the firm's finances. Essentially, he said he had been too busy to provide oversight regarding their activities, and had not asked the right questions that would have uncovered their deceptions. However, ultimate responsibility lies at the top of any organization, and Mr. Ebbers was found guilty and sentenced to 25 years in prison.

Failing to install and adhere to an ethical code of conduct for your organization. A company must have an effective ethics program that fairly represents the company's values and code of conduct. Such a program can be used to establish an effective ethical climate, maintain fairness and consistency in the handling of ethical issues over time, and help educate new employees as to expectations and performance standards. This educational component is especially important as workforces become more international and diverse. Employees that come from different cultural, educational, and family backgrounds need a common understanding of what is required by the business in ethical-related dealings. Ethics programs have been endorsed by the Federal Sentencing Guidelines for Organizations, and federal judges have been instructed to "go easy" on firms with extensive ethics compliance programs even when they incur a misstep. Ethics programs should include a compliance officer charged with making sure that employees live up to the ideals in the published code of conduct.

Research has shown that managers who work in more ethical organizations experience lower role conflict and role ambiguity than those who work in less ethical organizations. Role conflict adversely affects ethical behavioral intentions, while ethical culture both directly and indirectly affects ethical behavioral intentions.

Favoring One Stakeholder Group Over Another. Stakeholders are considered to be groups of people who have a "stake" in the success of the business. Those who put up the investment capital are called shareholders, and represent one stakeholder group; other stakeholders include employees, customers, suppliers, communities in which   businesses operate, and society in general. All stakeholders should benefit from a healthy, growing business, and the rights and obligations of all these stakeholders should be respected as ethical decisions are made. Good ethical decisions should benefit all groups. Poor ethical decisions favor one group at the expense of another.

Shareholders are very interested in the financial health and profitability of the firm, as the value of their investment increases when earnings per share increase. Consequently, through an elected board of directors, they tend to apply pressure to the firm to establish objectives to increase profitability sooner rather than later. These short-term objectives are important when they provide benchmarks along the path toward achieving long-term strategic initiatives, and they serve to rally both leadership and employees to achieve concentrated effort and attention. But striving to achieve short-term goals can backfire, if other stakeholder groups are ignored in the process. For instance, a plan to increase the short term profitability (benefiting shareholders) by decreasing employee benefits (adversely affecting employees), or increasing factory emissions (adversely affecting the community around the factory) may not be ethical. One may win the battle, so to speak, but lose the war.

"Chainsaw Al" Dunlap, who earned his nickname by cutting labor and administrative costs from troubled companies, was hired as CEO of Sunbeam Corporation in 1996 and given the charge to turn-around this venerable maker of kitchen appliances. In order to make sure that short-term sales objectives were consistently met, he instituted a "bill and hold" program in which retailers were encouraged to order merchandise for future delivery and payment. These orders were recorded as sales on Sunbeam's income statement, which inflated Sunbeam's reported revenues and profits. While this practice is technically legal, Dunlap ignored his obligation to inform investors and the board of directors about what he was doing. When the "bill and hold" program was discovered, shareholders sued the company and the stock price fell. As a result, "Chainsaw Al" was given the "axe" by the Sunbeam board.

Framework for Understanding Executive Ethical Decision-Making

It is easy for us to look at those convicted and serving time in prison for ethical misconduct, and dismiss them all as crooks, greedy, or just "bad" people. We can easily rationalize that if we had been in their situations, we would have acted differently and not have committed the ethical violations that caused their downfall. Unfortunately, this attitude may be a dangerous rationalization. Yes, some were greedy and sought their own interests from the beginning. But most of the rest were basically good people and accomplished executives, who tried to do the right thing. It wasn't for lack of good intentions that they failed. Why did they fail? Most failed because they paid too little attention to how ethical decisions should be made in their organizations. Without a good understanding of ethical decision-making, any of us could fall victim to the same errors.

A framework for Ethical Decision-Making is presented as Figure 1-1. It is based upon the understanding that ethical decisions in business are strongly influenced by the personal ethical standards of the

Figure 1-1

Framework for Understanding Ethical Decision-Making
Adapted from Ferrell, Fraedrich and Ferrell (2005)

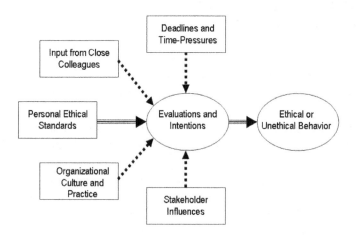

key decision-maker, and are moderated by other factors including organizational culture, input from colleagues, time pressures, and stakeholder influences. All of these factors may influence the decision-maker, resulting in an action (or non-action) that may be considered ethical or unethical. This framework is discussed in more detail in the following paragraphs.

Business leaders are constantly observing what is going on around them, evaluating the performance of their employees, observing the reactions of key customers, and looking for opportunities to enhance the performance of their organization as new challenges are confronted. This monitoring activity compares what is happening with the leader's view of what should be happening. When activities are observed that are unexpected or leading in the
wrong direction, the leader is moved to take action that overcomes the "wrong condition" and attempts to restore everything to a "right condition." This process of restoration is called decision-making. When questions about rights and obligations are involved in the decision, the process is called ethical decision-making.

As a result of prior education, family environment, religious training, life experience, and job expectations, business leaders develop a strong personal sense of right and wrong. This personal ethical sense affects which business conditions are dealt with and which are singled out for decision-making. Other factors that influence the decision are the organization's ethical culture, the time pressures involved in making and communicating decisions, performance pressures exerted by key stakeholders, and the influence of trusted colleagues and advisors. All of these factors play a role in determining when and how the business leader responds in an ethical decision situation.

For instance, suppose that you are the CEO of a major oil refining company during a period when OPEC supply decisions and rising world demand are pushing crude oil prices up sharply. So far, your firm has responded by increasing prices so that your profit margins are maintained in spite of the higher costs for crude, and as a result your firm is enjoying record profits. Suppose further that you read a *Wall Street Journal* article that reports that higher fuel prices are impacting the spending habits of American consumers and that auto manufacturers are laying off thousands of workers because consumers are opting to purchase smaller, fuel efficient vehicles instead of the larger, gas guzzling SUV's that they had expected to sell. You realize that you could temporarily reduce your prices resulting in a consumer savings of 10%, even while you achieve your profit forecast for the year.

Applying this example to the decision framework, you would rely on your personal sense of right and wrong to determine if easing the plight of consumers and auto workers was an issue that merited your consideration. Further, you might look at your company's culture and past company decisions to see if there is any precedent to addressing this type of issue. You might also look at all the other issues facing the company and   their respective priorities before you decide to spend the time needed to undertake an in-depth examination of a possible pricing change. You certainly would be concerned about the likely response of company shareholders, community groups, and employee groups should a price reduction decision be announced, so you probably would talk to individuals representing those groups to get their input. Finally, you would likely consult with trusted economists, political advisors, and other executives within the firm before making an informed decision.

What Happens When Ethical Decision-Making is Unethical?

When business leaders make poor ethical decisions, there are adverse consequences that impact the leader, the organization, and society as a whole. After a poor ethical decision is made, there may be a long time before any adverse consequence is apparent. This time lag may provide a false sense of security, and increase the leader's willingness to continue making decisions with the same shortcomings as the previous decision. When the adverse consequence finally arrives, as it surely will, there is a whole string of poor ethical behavior that must be evaluated. This exacerbates the problems created and increases the financial and organizational costs in correcting any problems.

The personal costs of ethical violations among leaders in American corporations should not be minimized. Guilty verdicts can profoundly alter the personal lives of executives, tear-apart their families and ruin their financial wealth. Court cases can drag on for many years, and consume fortunes in legal expenses. Unethical actions by leaders at the top of the firm can infect entire organizations, encouraging others to mimic the same behaviors, and result in loss of resources, employment levels, consumer and investor confidence, and bankruptcy. Finally, society is injured severely when others in society emulate the unethical proclivities of business leaders, and unethical behavior becomes more widespread throughout the workplace, entertainment, institutions and government.

The Benefits of Good Ethical Decision-Making

There are significant benefits to good ethical decision-making. First and foremost, many research studies have con-firmed what should be obvious -- that there is a positive and significant relationship between organization ethicality and organization performance. Companies that develop an ethi-cal code of conduct and follow it are financially more suc-cessful than those companies that don't. Companies that treat customers, employees, suppliers, or society unethically are not successful long term. They can fool people for a short while, but eventually ethical violations are uncovered and the glare of adverse public opinion takes its toll.

This book is all about how good ethical business decisions are made. It is based on the idea that leaders of business organizations (and those aspiring to become leaders someday) need basic guidance and education so that they increase their "batting average" in making good ethical decisions on the job. Furthermore, this book is based on the idea that good ethical practices can be taught. There are standards of performance that are discernable, make good business sense, and will assist leaders in making better decisions. Finally, this book is based upon the fact that personal ethical standards can and should have a significant influence on the business decisions made by that individual. Just as an organization is an extension of individual action, business ethics is an extension of personal ethics. What is right and what is wrong is consistent whether we are dealing with individual or organizational action.

The remainder of the book is organized in the following manner. In chapter two, we begin by examining the concept of "natural law" as a basis for truth in ethical decision-making. Then in chapter three, we explore some ideas of the great philosophers, and we examine the value of what they had to say as a guide for ethical consistency. In chapter four, we explore the nature and purpose of business enterprise for implications regarding ethical decision-making. In chapter five, we examine the law as an ethical threshold to corporate behavior. Finally, in chapter six, we propose an ethical roadmap that business leaders may follow to improve the ethical performance of their businesses.

Summary

1. In the past several years, the United States has witnessed a significant number of ethical violations on the part of high-profile corporate leaders.

2. The reasons for these lapses include: (1) undeveloped personal ethical standards; (2) leaving own personal ethical standards at home; (3) insufficient input from col-

leagues; (4) yielding to time pressures in making incomplete or sub-optimal decisions; (5) failing to install and adhere to an ethical code of conduct; and (6) favoring one stakeholder group over others.

3. A framework for Ethical Decision-Making is presented that suggests that ethical decisions in business are strongly influenced by the personal ethical standards of the key decision-maker together with organizational culture, input from colleagues, time pressures, and stakeholder influences.

4. Ethical missteps are expensive for the executive, the company and society; ethical firms are more successful than unethical firms.

2

An "Owner's Manual" for Human Interaction

Justin was pleased that he had found a roomy rental house close to campus. It had everything he wanted, including an eat-in kitchen with extra-large refrigerator, a living room big enough to play ping pong, and a shaded back yard patio for entertaining. But there was one catch: he had agreed to keep the yard mowed as part of the lease. When the grass reached knee high, he figured he better try out the lawn mower he found parked in the rear of the garage. After filling the tank with gasoline, he pulled on the rope to start the engine, but it wouldn't start. He examined the dip stick to check the oil level, and found only a small glob of black goop at the very bottom of the stick. Obviously, the crankcase was low on oil.

He looked around the garage for a can of oil, and finding none, he contemplated whether he should drive over to Wal-Mart to buy a quart. But then he started thinking. Why spend the money on oil, when all I need to do is to dilute the dried-up oil already in the crankcase? Let's see….Isn't gasoline a refined version of oil? Why not pour a little gasoline into the crank-case and see what happens? So he poured some gas into the crankcase and after a few pulls on the starter rope, the engine came to life and he began to mow. Unfortunately, the engine soon was making clanking noises and in a few minutes more it stopped completely, never to run again.

What happened? The gasoline had acted as a solvent to clean the oil from the engine's internal components. Without lubrication, the engine bearings had overheated, and the engine was ruined. Had Justin been able to find and read a copy of the owner's manual provided by the manufacturer when it was purchased, he would have seen the warning written in bold-face type: "Do not put anything into the crankcase except motor oil that meets SAE specifications." This was just one of many rules, requirements and safety warnings included in the manual, all intended to provide the user with guidance to maximize the useful life of the equipment. After this incident, Justin wished that he had sought out a copy of the owner's manual and had read the warnings. Now, his next trip to Wal-Mart was considerably more expensive because he had to buy a new lawnmower!

Manufacturers routinely provide owner's manuals for their products, either by including a printed copy, CD or DVD at the time of product purchase, or by mounting it on the firm's Website where owners may access it when needed. Good consumers pay attention to the guidelines, rules and warnings contained in these manuals. Anytime there is a problem or question about the operation of the product, they refer to the owner's manual for advice. After all, the maker of the product generally knows how the product is best used and maintained because it knows how it works. Justin learned his lesson. He resolved to pay attention to owner's manuals in the future and follow the recommended rules and guidelines.

The "Natural Law"

On July 4th, 1776, the first Congress of the United States issued the "unanimous Declaration of the thirteen united States of America," and this became the founding document of our nation. The first sentence of this declaration refers to the "Laws of Nature and of Nature's God," and subsequent sentences establish that citizens have the right to change government when that government allows those natural laws to be violated (Figure 2-1). Obviously, the concept of natural law was

Figure 2-1

The Beginning of the Declaration of Independence

IN CONGRESS, JULY 4, 1776
The unanimous Declaration of the thirteen united States of America

When in the Course of human events it becomes necessary for one people to dissolve the political bands which have connected them with another and to assume among the powers of the earth, the separate and equal station to which the Laws of Nature and of Nature's God entitle them, a decent respect to the opinions of mankind requires that they should declare the causes which impel them to the separation.

We hold these truths to be self-evident, that all men are created equal, that they are endowed by their Creator with certain unalienable Rights, that among these are Life, Liberty and the pursuit of Happiness. — That to secure these rights, Governments are instituted among Men, deriving their just powers from the consent of the governed, — That whenever any Form of Government becomes destructive of these ends, it is the Right of the People to alter or to abolish it, and to institute new Government, laying its foundation on such principles and organizing its powers in such form, as to them shall seem most likely to effect their Safety and Happiness.

deemed to be very important to the founding fathers as it was used to justify the separation of the colonies from the British Empire and the subsequent establishment of a new and separate nation. So, what is meant by natural law?

Just as the manufacturer of Justin's lawn mower built certain capabilities and limitations into that device which necessitates rules of use, the founders of our nation believed that the Creator of the human race built-in certain capabilities and limitations into our nature which require certain rules of conduct. When those rules are not obeyed, then humans and society suffer adverse consequences. Accordingly, natural law is really an ordering to our true good and consists of *the insights of human conduct and behavior that our Creator has built into our nature*. When we follow the inclinations of the natural law, we are aligning our lives according to the reason for our existence. Natural law is both universal and immutable. Its precepts apply to everyone – the entire human race – because each of us is bound to comply with the universal order as designed by the Creator. Since this law is woven into our very nature, the law commands and forbids with the same force everywhere and always. In essence, natural law is the "owner's manual" that prescribes rules of conduct for the human condition.

With this owner's manual, we should have assurance about what is right and wrong in our dealings with all those we meet. By following its precepts, we can do "good" while eliminating the "bad" from our lives. Through attentive knowledge of the natural law, we can avoid making stupid mistakes and damaging ourselves and those around us. But where, you ask, can we pick up a copy of this owner's manual? The hospital doesn't seem to send a copy home with each new baby, do they?

Written in Our Hearts?

The idea of decent behavior seems to be obvious to everyone. The ancient Egyptians, Babylonians, Chinese, Greeks, and Romans all produced similar written codes detailing laws

about what is right and wrong when it comes to human interaction. Some have spoken about the law being "written in our
hearts." The human is gifted with a desire to seek and know
truth, and life's evidence shows that when each one of us takes
the time to ponder the central questions about our existence,
we find at least an outline of the answers lurking somewhere
deep inside us. What we find is termed the "natural law," also
referred to as law of human nature, the moral law, the law of
fair play, decency, morality, or rule of equitable behavior. To
be clear, the natural law is not anything like an instinct. In-
stincts provide automatic responses and do not require the use
of reason. When the fast ball is sailing toward your head, your
instinct informs you to duck quickly! But the natural law works
differently. It does not command an automatic response, but
rather it causes us to contemplate, weigh alternatives and decide before we undertake action.

What does it mean that these laws are "written on our
hearts?" It means they correspond to our rightly ordered desires. Philosophers, poets and saints have suggested that mankind generally desires to do good and avoid evil. When we do
good we live well, and when we do bad we do not live well. We
have freedom always to follow or not follow the natural law,
but this is akin to our freedom to smoke, binge drink, stuff
ourselves, etc. We can do these things but if we do them we
are not going to be healthy.

Historically, respect for the natural law has been a subject
of concern for people of all religions, and much effort has
been put forward to educate and encourage followers regarding this concept. Christians and Jews believe that the Creator
did not leave it for each of us to discern the law by ourselves.
Rather, God reminded us by writing the essence of the natural
law in "Ten Words" or "Commandments" on two stone tablets
and giving them to the prophet Moses on Mount Sinai (Figure 2-2). Judeo-Christian tradition suggests that the first tablet
contains commandments that prescribe how we are to show
love to our Creator, including prohibitions against worshiping

strange gods, worshiping graven images, taking God's name in vain and setting aside one day each week for rest and worship. The second tablet prescribes how we are to relate to one another in this world. These "second" commandments include ordinances regarding respect for authority, equitable treatment of others, chastity in speech and behavior, property ownership rights, truth, and self control.

The "Second Tablet"

The first tablet commands are distinctively Judeo-Christian. But you don't have to be a Jew or a Christian to appreciate the second tablet commands, as there is a remarkable degree of agreement among the world's religions regarding these rules of conduct. Every one of these commandments is supported in the teachings and writings reverenced by the major religions of the world (Figure 2-3). For instance, the Qur 'an, which Muslims believe is the word of God as revealed to Mohammed, contains similarly-worded versions of each commandment. Buddhists advocate the "Ten Charges" and "Laws of Manu," Hindus advocate the "Tenfold Law," and Jainists advocate the "Ten Duties," all of which include ordinances which are consistent with the second tablet commandments of the Bible. These commandments are so universal, that even those who do not follow a particular faith usually acknowledge that they present wise and valuable counsel, the kind of advice that rises to the level of universal "common sense." In addition, these second tablet commands have had a profound influence on the development of law in the United States of America.

Figure 2-2

**The Ten Commandments
(Exodus 20:2-17; RSV)**

"I am the LORD your God, who brought you out of the land of Egypt, out of the house of bondage. You shall have no other gods before me. You shall not make for yourself a graven image, or any likeness of anything that is in heaven above, or that is in the earth beneath, or that is in the water under the earth; you shall not bow down to them or serve them; for I the LORD your God am a jealous God, visiting the iniquity of the fathers upon the children to the third and the fourth generation of those who hate me, but showing steadfast love to thousands of those who love me and keep my commandments. You shall not take the name of the LORD your God in vain; for the LORD will not hold him guiltless who takes his name in vain. Remember the Sabbath day, to keep it holy. Six days you shall labor, and do all your work; but the seventh day is a Sabbath to the LORD your God; in it you shall not do any work, you, or your son, or your daughter, your manservant, or your maidservant, or your cattle, or the sojourner who is within your gates; for in six days the LORD made heaven and earth, the sea, and all that is in them, and rested the seventh day; therefore the LORD blessed the Sabbath day and hallowed it. Honor your father and your mother, that your days may be long in the land which the LORD your God gives you. You shall not kill. You shall not commit adultery. You shall not steal. You shall not bear false witness against your neighbor. You shall not covet your neighbor's house; you shall not covet your neighbor's wife, or his manservant, or his maidservant, or his ox, or his ass, or anything that is your neighbor's."

Figure 2-3

Natural Law Precepts in World Religions

	Buddhism	Christianity	Hinduism	Islam	Jainism	Judaism
Honesty	●	●	●	●	●	●
Fair Treatment	●	●	●	●	●	●
Self Control	●	●	●	●	●	●
Priority Setting	●	●	●	●	●	●
Protection of Life	●	●	●	●	●	●
Respect for Authority	●	●	●	●	●	●
Property Ownership	●	●	●	●	●	●

The second tablet commandments include:

Honor your father and your mother. This command engenders respect for all legitimate authority, beginning with one's parents, and forbids doing anything against, or failing to give honor and duty to those in authority positions. Our laws regarding equity, regulatory compliance, pensions, and medical assistance for the elderly were all influenced by this commandment.

You shall not kill. This implies that persons should undertake all lawful endeavors to preserve and protect their own life and the life of others; while forbidding the unjust taking of human life. Our laws regarding murder, manslaughter, suicide, assisted suicide and abortion are all related to this commandment, as are laws relating to the care of the sick, suffering and impoverished in our society.

You shall not commit adultery. This command-ment not only requires respect for the marriage bond, but requires the protection of chastity in speech and behavior. Our laws regarding pornography, indecency, and marriage reflect this idea.

You shall not steal. This commandment recognizes the property rights of individuals, and prohibits the taking of others' lawfully gained wealth. Our laws related to copyrights, patents, real and personal property, and estates all reflect this commandment.

You shall not bear false witness against your neighbor. This commandment requires maintaining and promoting truth among people, and enjoins anything that is injurious to someone's good name. Our laws relating to libel, slander, truth in advertising and promotional communications reflect this commandment.

You shall not covet your neighbor's wife or your neighbor's goods. These commands require self-control in dealings with others, and prohibit scheming, fraud or deceit in trying to obtain what belongs to someone else. These commands are especially applicable to business leaders. Our laws regarding fair competition are partially based upon controlling covetousness.

Taken together, the second tablet commands provide an effective summary of the "natural law." These commands provide support for the constitutional rights of equal dignity, respect and worth for each human being. The commandments imply fair and equitable treatment for all. To be sure, even though there is broad agreement on the commandments themselves, societies have entertained disagreements as to interpretation and application in different contexts. These varied interpretations are the principal reason we see differences in the rights and obligations of citizens in different nations, and disagreements as to what the right course of action might be in specific situations.

Are these Laws Moral Absolutes?

Some argue that these laws are moral absolutes as our nation's founders did, while others suggest that there are no absolutes, not even in the natural law. Such is the case for the moral relativist philosophy we will discuss in greater detail in chapter three. Moral relativists propose that the commandments in the natural law should never be taken as absolutes. After all, they argue, our world is a complex place and there are so many things to consider in any moral decision. Reliance on guidelines written 3000 years ago is not being objective. Obviously there are always extenuating circumstances that prevent anything from being considered an absolute. Relativists usually follow with an example provided as an illustration, such as the two that follow:

Suppose your father was Adolf Hitler. You certainly wouldn't honor him despite the implications of the "honor your father and mother" command. Adolf Hitler does not deserve honor! Or, suppose a thug walked through the door of a classroom with an AK47 machine gun and announced he would kill you and everyone else in the class unless you lied about his identity. You couldn't be expected to tell the truth about him despite the "Do Not Bear false Witness" command. Therefore, there is no such thing as a moral absolute.

Moral idealists, however, effectively counter the relativist's argument, and propose that the commands in the natural law do rise to the stature of moral absolutes. Yes, they acknowledge that human interaction is complicated, but the natural law provides a foundation of constancy and truth that can be relied upon no matter what the situation. Natural law is absolute because it is based on insight into what a human being is. No matter who you are, whenever you put gas in the crankcase, you will wreck the engine, because it is contrary to the nature of the engine. Similarly, if you do hardcore drugs you will wreck your brain, and if you act contrary to the natural law you will do harm to the well-being of yourself and others.

The disagreement is analogous to the question of whether the glass is half empty or half full – in other words, where is the starting point? The relativist begins with an empty glass (i.e., the moral law doesn't apply to the situation at hand), then gradually adds parts of the law when it seems advantageous to him to do so. The moral idealist begins with a full glass (i.e., the moral law does apply), and only mitigates its use when two or more applicable moral laws are placed in conflict.

Each of the situations described above is constructed so that in obeying one moral command another command is violated. Ethical dilemmas are frequently like this. In such situations, one must use intelligence and reason to decide how to obey the commands that are placed in opposition by the specific situation. Consequently, it may not be appropriate to honor Adolf Hitler (even if he were your father), if by doing so you were required to misrepresent the truth about his life. And in the second example, it may be readily appropriate to convey a falsehood, if in doing so you prevent the violation of the "Do not kill" command and save the lives of a whole room full of people.

The Ten Commandments didn't come with numbers on them, and in Jesus' time, people were wondering which commands dealing with how we relate to our neighbors were the more important ones and which were less important. By knowing how they ranked, people would be able to more readily come to an agreement when dealing with ethical dilemmas of the type we've discussed. In fact, a lawyer even asked Jesus to name the greatest of the commandments. Presumably, he planned to continue his line of questioning with "What's the next greatest commandment, and the next?" until he had Jesus rank-order all ten. However, Jesus answered in a way that put a stop to further inquiry. His reply was, "You shall love the Lord your God with all your heart, with all your soul and with all your mind. This is the great and first commandment. And a second is like it. You shall love your neighbor as yourself. On these two commandments depend all the law and the prophets." [Matt. 22:36-40]

In effect, Jesus told the lawyer that there was unity between the first tablet commands (how we go about loving God) with the second tablet commands (how we go about loving each other). Thus, Christian tradition holds that the first group of commands is fundamental in establishing a right relationship with our neighbor. Christianity teaches that when you love God, you will receive the encouragement and fortitude necessary to really love your neighbor as yourself. In so doing, you are given the power and fortitude to obey the second tablet commands.

Other religions convey similar perspectives about the unity between love of Creator and love of neighbor; at the same time, they maintain agreement on the essential commands in the natural law. World religions do hold differing perspectives about the nature of the Creator and what we should be doing to maintain a right relationship. Consequently, there is a rich diversity in religious practices.

and ways to worship in the United States and around the world. After experiencing the stifling effects of state-sponsored religion present in the colonies while under British rule, our nation's founding fathers promoted the free exercise of religion by including the "establishment clause" in the constitution. This made it unlawful for government to establish a religion, and thereby allowed personal religious choice among its citizens.

Religion performs an important function in that it helps inform individual consciences as to interpretation and application of the natural law. Each religion provides an internally consistent and systematic understanding of what is most important in one's life. The practice of one's faith leads to a systematic understanding that becomes second nature, and helps each individual become more effective in making good decisions regarding the ethical dilemmas they face. Diversity in religious belief is a tremendous asset to this nation, because it helps inform social consciousness and political discussion.

Organizations as Extensions of Individuals

The history of the human race demonstrates that humans frequently join together into groups – families, villages, social and charitable organizations, businesses, companies, states and nations. Each of these organizations has a purpose, and each is formed because the group can be more effective or more efficient in accomplishing the purpose set forth than an individual acting alone could. Organizations are formed of individuals and are always agents of collective individual action. Accordingly, because natural law applies to individuals, it applies to organizations by extension. That's why our nation's founders were so upset with the British government. When measured against the natural law, the British government was "stealing" the personal property of the citizens in the thirteen colonies through its practice of "taxation without representation."

All organizations, no matter what their purpose, are expected to obey the natural law. A firm that deceives its investors and customers, or falsifies information provided to government agencies, or produces unsafe products that could harm those who use them, violates the natural law. Leaders of these organizations have the same obligation that our founding fathers had. Any violations of the natural law should be identified and corrected immediately. If the organization somehow persists in the violation, the leader should declare his or her independence from that organization and move to another one that respects the commands of the natural law.

Public Display of the Ten Commandments

In 2005, two lawsuits were decided by the U. S. Supreme Court regarding the display of the Ten Commandments on public property. Opponents argued that such display constitutes the endorsement of a particular religious faith system, and therefore is a violation of the establishment clause in the constitution which enjoins the government from establishing a religion. Proponents argued that such display is consistent with the Judeo-Christian tradition of the United States, and is essentially historical in nature, because the legal system is firmly based on several of the ideas presented in the Ten Commandments. The Court was swayed by both arguments. In one case they ruled that the display was unconstitutional because the composition and nature of the display served an essentially religious purpose. But in the other case, the display was allowed to stand as it's presence was deemed as essentially historical in nature. Accordingly, the purpose of the display seems to be the over-riding factor in deciding whether it is permitted. It is interesting to note that objections to displaying the Ten Commandments have not been based upon the veracity or applicability of the laws contained therein, but rather the implied religious nature of its source. Had the same commandments been listed by Hamilton, Jefferson or Franklin on one of our founding documents, or had you or I written them into the covenants when founding our town, there would be little objection to displaying these ideas in the public square.

As a result of these recent decisions, the business leader should recognize that in some circumstances a display of the full Ten Commandments can be perceived by employees as endorsing a particular religious view. However, as demonstrated here, the ideas presented in the second tablet form the basis of the natural law, which has been almost universally accepted. Its use does not favor a particular religious perspective or promote one denomination over another, and it would indeed be unfortunate if someone would "throw the baby out with the bath water." Businesses can and should refer to the insights contained in the second tablet in developing and communicating codes of ethics for their organizations. Business decisions are made by individuals, and those individuals cannot be good decision-makers if they leave their moral sense at home.

Summary

1. Just as a manufacturer builds certain capabilities and limitations into a product that necessitates rules of use, the Creator of the human race builds

2. certain capabilities and limitations into our nature which requires rules of conduct. Those rules are called the "natural law."

3. There is broad agreement across world religions that the commands contained in the second tablet of the "Ten Words" given to Moses, constitute ideas that are contained in the natural law. These include honesty, fair treatment, self-control, priority setting, protection of life, respect for authority and property ownership.

4. The commands of the natural law can be treated as "moral absolutes." Ethical dilemmas occur when the situation at hand places two laws in opposition, and require intelligence and reasoning to decide a course of action that reconciles the conflict.

5. All organizations, no matter what their purpose, are expected to obey the natural law. Any violations to the natural law should be corrected immediately.

6. The natural law does not favor one particular religious perspective or promote one denomination over another.

3

Perspectives on Ethical Thought

Traditionally, philosophers have distinguished between *ethics* and *morals*. Ethics refers to the systematic science of right and wrong human conduct. Morals, or morality, describes the actual patterns of right and wrong conduct, or said another way, the direct application of rules of morals in action. Without morals, ethics would be incomplete – an empty shell.

Consequently, the terms ethics and morals, although often used interchangeably, are really not the same. Ethics provides a structure of knowledge (an ethical theory or system), but individuals will likely make their own decision based on personal morals as applied to the facts and circumstances in any particular case. Similarly, society will tend to make societal decisions based on the collective personal morals of the population.

Figure 3-1 illustrates a three-step process that demonstrates how an ethical system and morals application relates to decision-making. A particular ethical system, such as relativism, is first adopted by the decision- maker as a framework for action. The decision-maker then

Figure 3-1

Ethics, Morals and Decision Relationships

ETHICAL SYSTEM

(Example: Relativism [Protagoras] – No objective standard.
Man *is the measure of all things*.)

MORALS APPLICATION

(Subjective feelings and beliefs of the individual
applied to factual situation.)

DECISION
(Decision based on Morals Application)

Figure 3-2

Ethical Relativism Decision-Making in Action

ETHICAL SYSTEM (Relativism)

Ethical Issue: Should I turn the lights off at the office after
work? I will determine and measure right and wrong.

MORALS APPLICATION

Subjective feeling/belief whether right or wrong to turn the
lights off. The boss/company has mistreated and underpaid
me. The boss/company should be punished.

DECISION

Leave the lights on. Although small, the boss/company will
suffer/be punished in the form of higher electrical expenses
for underpaying and mistreating me. I am right.

applies his or her subjective moral beliefs to the facts at hand, weighs those facts, and then reaches a decision. Suppose Renée is an environmentally conscious person. She drives a gas/electric hybrid vehicle and is normally meticulous about recycling waste. At home, she is quick to turn off lights when she leaves a room so as to conserve electricity. But at her place of work, it is a different matter. Figure 3-2 illustrates the three-step decision-making procedure that Renée uses in making a decision on how to behave. This example is based upon relativism, but there are many more ethical systems that can be applied.

Throughout history, ethical thought and reflective analysis have been the subject of many writings, books and publications. Philosophers have developed various ethical theories aimed at assisting decision-makers in making sound decisions. A review of these contributions together with their limitations is instructive for any student of business ethics. Following are eight common theories of ethics, presented in historical order.

PROTAGORAS – Relativism

Protagoras (481-411 B.C.), the Greek philosopher whose teachings formed the foundation of the ethical theory of relativism, was made famous by his statement, "Man is the measure of all things." His relativism theory proposed that all values or judgments differ according to circumstances, persons and cultures. Relativism refuses to accept that any belief is ever objectively true or false. The issue of correctness of two or more conflicting points of view would be moot because the held belief would be correct for the person or society who espoused it and equally correct for the person or society who rejected it.

Relativism argues that everything is relative to everything else. Relativism determines an ethically correct decision or behavior in relation to the ethical belief held by the individual or group. If the individual holds the belief that the ethical decision he makes is correct, then it is correct. Likewise, if a society has a certain belief that a specific course of human action is acceptable and right, then it is ethical within that particular society. The ethical relativist satisfies and conforms to his own moral standard by deciding what he believes is right and consequently, because he adheres to and believes in this moral standard, he cannot be challenged that he is wrong. It is his moral standard because his subjective belief and feelings dictate this standard to him.

For example, if Sandra believes that lying about the financial condition of the business firm is acceptable behavior if the lie will assist the firm in obtaining a lucrative contract, then this lie would be ethical for her. Or, if Brett believes that the making and taking of bribes to secure business contracts is good practice, then it is ethical for him. Sometimes societies approve of activities which are considered ethical within that particular society, but maybe not outside the society. For example, a certain society may approve of and practice euthanasia. The practice is looked upon as ethical within that particular society, but other societies may consider the practice unethical.

The individual moral standard is the ethical standard for relativism and the individual moral standard varies widely from person to person and may change from time to time. Accordingly, relativism is like shifting sand (the recommended course of action changes all the time) and the ethics of the relativist lack an objective moral standard.

PLATO – Virtue and Knowledge

The ancient Greek philosopher, *Plato* (427-347 B.C.), was one of the most important ethics scholars in the history of Western culture. His virtue and knowledge theory was based on the proposition that at the core of every person's being was the desire to achieve happiness in life. He believed that although people try to act in ways that make them happy, often the result in unhappiness. He reasoned that unhappiness occurs because people are mistaken about the proper actions needed to produce happiness. Plato proposed that a healthy soul was the key to individual happiness, and without a healthy soul, no one could experience true happiness.

In order to achieve a healthy soul, Plato taught that moral virtue is of paramount importance. Moral virtue is defined as conforming to the "   standard of right." The virtuous person adheres to the standard of right while the non-virtuous person does not. In order to be virtuous, the individual has to have the desire to be virtuous. Plato reasoned that individuals do not try to be virtuous because they do not realize that true virtue produces true happiness.

Accordingly, lack of knowledge is a fundamental problem in ethical behavior, and people do not know that adherence to the "standard of right" produces true happiness in their lives. So, what is the solution? Plato suggested that people should be taught how virtuous behavior leads to a healthful soul and true personal happiness. Since everyone wants to be happy, if they have knowledge to act virtuously, they will act virtuously. So, if Renée, Sandra and Brett chose to adopt Plato's virtue theory of ethics, they may decide to apply the virtues of justice and honesty in the situations described. Renée would turn off the lights both at home and work, Sandra would tell the truth, and Brett would stop offering bribes.

ARISTOTLE – Function Fulfillment

Aristotle (384-322 B.C.) was a student of Plato, and was significantly influenced by his teacher. The two are generally viewed as the two most influential Greek philosophers. Like Plato, Aristotle believed that happiness is the goal of all human beings and that virtue was paramount to ethical behavior. He argued that sufficient knowledge empowers people to act in a proper manner
and to live happy lives. But wealth, possessions, honors, and titles are all inadequate – they do not lead to true happiness.

Rather true happiness must be self-sufficient, final and attainable. A self-sufficient life is one that is desirable, totally enjoyable and lacks nothing. The finality is perfect and desirable in and of itself and not for anyone else or the sake of something else. One must be able, without outside assistance, to personally attain the ultimate desire. Aristotle maintained that happiness, and only happiness, is the goal which satisfies all three of these requirements.

To achieve happiness, the individual must fulfill his or her function in life. Of course, in order to fulfill one's function in life, one must first determine what they do best. The function of all human beings is to reason, so according to Aristotle, a happy life is one governed by reason. To behave ethically, one must be virtuous which necessarily includes the ability to reason. To behave unethically is to demonstrate moral imperfection and thus, imperfect reasoning. Aristotle espoused that moral virtue occurs when extremes are avoided and means are adhered to. For example, if one assumes that courage is a virtue, when does it begin and end? Using the extremes avoidance theory, the virtue of courage would occur on the mean somewhere between the undesirable characteristics of cowardice at one extreme and foolhardiness at the other extreme.

IMMANUEL KANT – Duty and Reason

The German philosopher, *Immanuel Kant* (1724-1804), proposed that doing one's duty is more important than being happy or making other people happy. The determination of duty is defined by reason. According to Kant, individuals have a universal obligation toward other human beings to act in a moral manner. This universal obligation cannot be ascertained by studying human desires to do good because human desires are different from person to person. He believed that the basis for morality in individuals was found in their rational nature, or their ability to reason, because the ability to reason is the same in everyone. Kant proposed that one's moral conscience reveals to every individual that moral precepts are not only universal, but also necessary.

Kant believed the good will of a person was essential for the achievement of some degree of happiness. But goodwill is not good because it achieves good results; it is good because goodwill seeks to do good. According to Kant, reasoning does not necessarily produce happiness, but reasoning is innately designed to produce goodwill in people. Goodwill is accomplished when one acts to fulfill a moral duty. Pure goodwill occurs when a moral duty is performed without self-interest on the part of the doer.

The theories of categorical and hypothetical imperatives were developed by Kant. Now, an imperative is something that is deemed mandatory. So Kant's categorical imperative stands for the proposition that individuals should govern their actions in relation to the consequences that would occur if everyone else acted in the same manner. Therefore, a person should act like he would expect other members of society to act. The categorical imperative is an unconditional directive which prescribes actions to be accomplished because of the moral worth of the act. By contrast, the hypothetical imperative directs what ought to be done for the achievement of a desired goal. For example, "One should testify truthfully in court as a matter of universal principle of telling the truth," is a categorical imperative. On the other hand, "One should testify truthfully in court to avoid being prosecuted for perjury," is a hypothetical imperative.

JOHN STUART MILL – Utilitarianism

The leading advocate of *utilitarianism* was Englishman John Stuart Mill (1806-1873) whose philosophy extended that of fellow Englishman Jeremy Bentham (1748-1832). The basic postulate of utilitarianism is that the object of morality is the enhancement of the greatest happiness of the greatest number of members of society. The doctrine of utilitarianism or utility morals is also commonly known as the Greatest Happiness Principle. This principle suggests that actions are right in proportion as they create or promote happiness, and actions are wrong if they create or promote unhappiness. Mill's theory defines happiness as pleasure and the absence of pain, whereas unhappiness is the absence of pleasure and the presence of pain. This morality postulate is grounded on the idea that pleasure and freedom from pain are the only things desirable as ultimate ends to mankind and that all desirable things are desirable either for the pleasure inherent in them, or as means to the enhancement of pleasure and the prevention of pain. Whatever action is best and causes happiness and thus, less pain, to the greatest number of individuals in society, is the correct moral action for one to take.

The outcome of the proposed action is contemplated for the greatest number of people. The thrust of utilitarianism is outcome oriented, that is, emphasis is on the consequences of the act. The nature of the act itself or preconceived ideals of morals are irrelevant. What matters is the greatest good for the greatest number. For example, if serving vanilla ice cream increased the happiness of   999 individuals whereas serving strawberry shortcake increased the happiness of 1000 individuals, the latter act would be judged the correct moral decision to make!

KARL MARX – Economic Morality

Prussian *Karl Marx* (1818-1883), considered the most successful social reformer of the 19th century, created the ethical theory of economic morality. He argued that morality is simply rationalizations structured by the ruling economic classes. As these ruling classes change, so does morality. According to Marx, an economic basis exists for all human institutions, thought and action. The intellectual, political and social development of the individual is conditioned and determined by the economic system under which he or she works or lives.

Because the ruling class controls the social economic system, it also controls the particular ideas and concepts of history, religion, art and philosophy that the people are exposed to. Marx argued that the moral ideas and standards put forth by traditional moral philosophers based on pure reason were in and of themselves incomplete, because moral ideas and standards are also subject to and influenced by the economic conditions of life.

Marx proclaimed that morality in general is meaningless. Every value judgment of right and wrong serves the interests of the particular social class at a given period of time. For example, he maintained that from the viewpoint of the working class, the economy of capitalism failed to serve their interests. Other classes, such as the class in power, would have a different perspective and, therefore, a different view on ethics. He characterized all morality as ideology and asserted that communists adhered to no morality. His ideal was a classless society free from the capitalist's greed for money and property. When society no longer has the structure of the classes, he surmised that the antagonism of classes toward each other would disappear. Because moral principles originate in class conflicts, when classes disappear, moral principles will no longer be needed or occupy any authoritative place in society.

FRIEDRICH NIETZSCHE – Modern Egoism

Friedrich Nietzsche (1844-1900), a Prussian native, declared that *God is dead* and invented the "transvaluation of values" doctrine. In holding up to ridicule the accepted ideals of the Judeo-Christian tradition, he described them as reversals of the true values of mankind. Nietzsche attacked what he perceived as the decadence and hypocrisy of traditional European morality, and predicted that traditional morality would lead to the destruction of western civilization.

Nietzsche called for a moral revolution through his transvaluation of values to save what he considered to be a weakening western civilization. His corrected table of virtues includ-

ed: pride instead of humility; contempt in place of sympathy
and pity; and tolerance in place of love of   one's   neighbor.
However, he did not intend his doctrine for the common
man but only for those who were intellectually capable of receiving it. In attempting to appeal to the intellectual aristocracy of
his day, Nietzsche exhorted them to prepare themselves to become *Supermen*, the highest and best stage in human development. The common man is surpassed in the superman who is
symbolic of the free spirit, proud of his magnificent physical
and mental strength and his own personal worth. The Superman theory departs from Darwin's evolution theory in that the
Superman achieves his mastery over nature and the environment and dominance over fellow humans by his will to power.
The determination of values is made by man alone.
Man passes judgment and requires no approval from any so-
called God or other man. Man as the creator of values honors
whatever he recognizes in himself. Morality is merely self-glo-
rification. Nietzsche argued that exploitation and competition
are characteristic of all living things because they are the essence of the will to power.

JEAN-PAUL SARTRE – Absolute Freedom

The French philosopher, *Jean-Paul Sartre* (1905-1980), created the ethical theory of *existentialism* whose central theme is
that *absolute freedom* is the condition of human existence. Because of this absolute freedom, humans are bound only by
the ideals and obligations which they dedicate for themselves.
According to the *existentialist*, there are no universal principles
to guide or sanction the conduct of man although human decisions impact the life of the decision-maker and perhaps those
around him. The order of society is nothing more than a fab-
rication because individuals exist in total isolation of others.

Who man is, is a function of what man chooses or wills.
Man is nothing until he exists; only afterward will he
be something, and only he himself will have made what he

will be. Therefore, man is nothing else but what he makes of himself. According to Sartre, absolute human freedom and the denial of the existence of God makes man solely responsible for his acts. Man is totally alone in his freedom with no excuses. So, like Protagoras' relativism, Sartre's existentialism lacks an objective standard of truth.

The Bottom Line on Ethical Philosophies

Students of ethical philosophers can choose which ever ethical theory best conforms to their own personal morals, and therein lies the basic problem. Which ethical theory should the individual follow? Is the same theory best for both the individual and society, or are separate theories best? Which theory should the business firm follow? Are ethical theories different for the individual, society and the business firm? Or, are ethics, or should ethics, be the same in all contexts? One way to resolve these questions is to look at alternate levels of goal-setting, as we do in the following section.

Goal Setting

The eight previously discussed ethical systems are just a small sampling of the large number of ethical philosophies which have been proposed over the years. The basic differences among each philosophy can be explained in terms of the level of goal setting determined by each philosopher. Four levels of goals are possible: (1) personal level goals; (2) group level goals; (3) society level goals and (4) transcendence level goals. These are summarized in Table 3-1.

At the first level, the individual strives to maximize self interest by doing "what's good for me." Nietzsche's Modern Egoism is a philosophy based at this first level,

Table 3-1

Four Levels of Goal Setting

Level 1	Objectives:	Maximize pleasure and Minimize Pain; gain advantage over others
"Do What's Good for Me"	Characteristics:	Obligation is to self alone. No desire for common, intrinsic, or ultimate good. Gratification is immediate. Negatives are lack of self-worth, fear of tangible loss/harm, boredom, jealousy, isolation and cynicism.
	Conceptual Foundation:	Nietzsche's Modern Egoism
Level 2	Objectives:	Integral part of successful group; gain advantage over other groups
"Do What's Good for My Group"	Characteristics:	Promotion of group is primary; personal power and control are key. Gratification is short-term. Negatives are fear of failure and uncontrolled competitiveness.
	Conceptual Foundations:	Protagoras' Relativism; Sartre's Existentialism

Table 3-1 (continued)

Four Levels of Goal Setting

Level 3	Objectives:	Do good beyond self.
"Do What's Good for the Majority"	Characteristics:	Principles include justice, love, and community. Intrinsic goodness is an end in itself. Decisions are focused on the greater good. Gratification tends to be longer term.
	Conceptual Foundations:	Mill's Utilitarianism and Marx' Economic Morality
Level 4	Objectives:	Participate in giving and receiving ultimate meaning, goodness, ideals and love.
"Do What's Best for Everyone"	Characteristics:	Good is ultimatized. Principles include ultimate truth, love, justice and beauty. Gratification is eternal.
	Conceptual Foundations:	Plato's Common Good, Aristotle's Functional Fulfillment, and Kant's Categorical Imperative

and insights from this philosophy might very well be beneficial if the goal is to win at a game of cards or other game involving individual players. But, it has limited applicability if the goal is to run a complex business.

At the second level, the goal is for "my team" to win, and philosophies directed at this level such as relativism and existentialism might provide the business leader with insights on how to select what's beneficial for the team. This level of goal setting might make sense if the object was to win the Olympic Gold Medal in hockey, for instance, but it is not very applicable for leaders of a business organization when that organization has expectations to deliver benefits to customer, suppliers, municipalities and those other than team members.

At the third level, the goal is to do good beyond self, so that others benefit. The basic decision rule is to do what's best for the majority – if more people profit from the action that those that lose, then the action is considered moral. Utilitarianism and economic morality are two moral philosophies that fit at this level. These approaches may provide insights into decision-making if you are a politician in a representative democracy, and they may provide some insights for business executives attempting to discern moral action when competing stakeholder groups do not benefit equally. Certainly, this level of goal setting is superior to the first two levels.

At the fourth level, the goal is to make decisions that correspond to giving and receiving ultimate truth, meaning, goodness, and love. In that way, decision-making respects what is best for not just one individual, one group or the majority of people; rather it reflects what is best for everyone. Plato's common good, Aristotle's functional fulfillment and Kant's categorical imperative correspond to this fourth level of goal setting. For the founders of our country and indeed, for most Americans today, ultimate truth and   meaning   was   defined, and   continues to be
defined, by our Creator. Consequently, when we do what God wants us to do, then we benefit all in his creation to the maxi-

mum extent possible. When we engage at this level of goal setting, good is ultimatized and gratification tends to become eternal. All business leaders should strive for decision-making based upon fourth level goals.

Contrary to what we see in the news media, decision- making should not revolve around conflict between the "rights" of one group versus the "rights" of another. Spirited conflict makes news and sells newspapers, and helps inform politicians about what issues in society need attention at the present time. Polling data can serve the purpose of helping assess what specific groups of people believe should be done. However, business organization decision-making is not about pitting one group against another; that's goal setting at the second level. Nor is it about polling the population to see what action they favor; that's goal setting at the third level. Good ethical decision-making in business situations is done at the fourth level, where the objective is to make balanced decisions that benefit everyone, not just for now, but in the future as well.

Let's apply these levels to an example. For instance, when an oil company prices its products, it could set the price so that current quarter profitability is maximized, thereby increasing the CEO's quarterly bonus compensation (level 1); or the firm could set the price so that shareholder dividends are maximized (level 2); or the firm could set the price so that the majority of shareholders and consumers are happy (level 3); or the firm could set the price so that consumers begin to exercise more conservation leading to reduced dependence on foreign oil sources and furthering the cause of world peace (level 4). Obviously, the level 4 alternative is the preferred course of action. It is the only action that attempts to achieve a lasting good.

This ethical journey leads us back to the fundamental expression of all laws for a society steeped in the Judeo-Christian tradition – the *Ten Commandments* or *Decalogue* – an ideal basis for ethical decision-making. When leaders of organizations strive to follow the rules presented in the Ten Commandments, they are automatically drawn to decision-making at the fourth level. As we discussed in Chapter 2, the second "tablet" of the Decalogue, that is the natural law, provides rules of conduct that are universal in scope. These rules of conduct are consistent with the teaching of the major religions of the world – *Christianity, Judaism, Buddhism, Hinduism* and *Islam*.

Figure 3-3 describes how there is always progression toward making correct ethical decisions when utilizing the inerrant natural law. On the other hand, the application of the ethics of human designs may involve errancy that results in making questionable ethical decisions.

Figure 3-3

Correct Ethical Decision-Making vs. Questionable or Incorrect Decision-Making

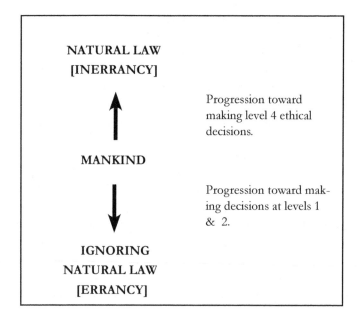

Summary

1. Ethics is a systematic science of right and wrong human conduct.

2. Numerous ethical systems have emerged throughout history, including Protagoras' Relativism, Plato's Virtue and Knowledge, Aristotle's Function Fulfillment, Kant's Duty and Reason, Mill's Utilitarianism, Marx's Economic Morality, Nietzsche's Modern Egoism and Sartre's Absolute Freedom.

3. Goal setting levels organize the ethical philosophers into four categories: a) do what's good for me; b) do what's good for my group; c) do what's good for the majority; and d) do what's best for everyone.

4. The "natural law" portion (the second tablet) of the Ten Commandments is consistent with the teachings of the major religions of the world – *Christianity, Judaism, Buddhism, Hinduism* and *Islam*—and defines universal rules of human conduct and interaction. The natural law corresponds to the fourth level of goal setting.

4

Dollars and Ethical Sense, Not Just Dollars and Cents

Who would have ever believed that the giant aircraft and prime defense contractor, Boeing Company, would have been implicated in the most sweeping Pentagon procurement fraud and scandal since the end of the Cold War? In yet another 2006 *Wall Street Journal* front page ethics-buster, previous high ranking corporate officers were sent off to federal prison for their unlawful and unethical roles in the illegal recruiting of a senior Air Force procurement official. This official had authority over billions of dollars in Boeing contracts and had improperly acquired proprietary documents of competitor Lockheed Martin Corporation for use in helping Boeing win a competition for government rocket-launching business.

In order to avoid criminal charges, Boeing agreed to pay $565 million to cover civil claims and $50 million to resolve criminal investigations. In the aftermath of the scandal, new CEO, Jim McNerney, announced a complete overhaul of Boeing's ethical culture. McNerney stated that previous management did not place enough emphasis on ethical behavior. As a consequence, McNerney discontinued an executive compensation plan under which executives were rewarded for meeting primarily financial goals. His new plan emphasizes integrity and ethical leadership.

To ensure compliance with Boeing's new ethical rules, settlement of the criminal and civil charges will require substantial outside oversight including mandatory reporting of results of any internal inquiries of ethical violations to the United States Justice Department. Clearly, unethical and apparently unlawful conduct has cost this company $615 million plus an incredible amount of damage to the corporate image. Being unethical can obviously cost any company a lot of money. Conversely, being ethical can be profitable, as we shall see later in this chapter.

Corporate Responsibility to Society

Because all businesses are a part of society, and as such, society, through its laws and regulations, permit businesses to exist, this relationship carries with it a duty on the part of all businesses to act in a responsible manner toward society. Several theories of business social responsibility have been developed and are discussed in the next section.

Profit Maximization is the basic, traditional social responsibility theory of all business. People go into business to make money. Ask any entrepreneur if they would rather make a profit of $500,000 or $600,000 from their business. Ask any employee if he would rather be paid $100,000 or $110,000 annual salary. The answer would always be the higher number. Why? Because maximizing profit is the very nature of business.

Maximizing profits allows businesses to accomplish a number of important functions. First of all, no business will survive very long without making a profit from its operations. It is a well-known fact that businesses operate in cycles. Some years are good; some years are lean. Maximizing profits allows a business to be better prepared for the lean years. Second, maximizing profits may be good for employees especially if it means that more money is available for wages and fringe benefits. Third, maximizing profits may be good for investors because high profitability increases return on investment. Investors are risk takers in that they have invested their capital at the risk of losing it, and they want their capital to work hard for them. They want their capital working at full capacity. Fourth, maximizing profits benefits society by keeping firms in business, keeping citizens gainfully employed and contributing to the overall economy and welfare of the nation.

The top priority in the profit maximization theory lies in the enhancement and protection of the owners of the business, be they sole proprietors, shareholders of a corporation, members of a limited liability company or other investors. After all, they are the real risk takers in that they have made a capital investment that they could lose if the business fails. Why assign them this highest priority of preference? Because there would be no business without their investment capital. If there was no business, there would be no employees, no products manufactured or services performed, no taxes collected, and no benefit to society. People would be out of work, and society would be harmed.

This theory holds that profit maximization of the firm is the only objective by which a firm fulfills its social responsibility (so long as the business operates within the bounds of the law). Further, according to this theory, the only duty of a business is to its owners and investors, and all other non-owner interests are irrelevant.

The maximization of profit to the exclusion of all other interests is clearly a much too restrictive view of corporate social responsibility. While it is true that a company must be profitable in order to continue in business, the interests of employees, the environment, suppliers, the community, and others with a pertinent relationship with the business should not be minimized or ignored. For example, suppose that the loyal employees of a company have been without a pay raise for several years, and management has been promising a raise when company financial conditions permit. Suppose further that the company has earned record profits for the last three years, but this year management again chooses to reward the investors with record returns instead of providing a pay raise for employees. As a result, management has broken its promises and denied pay raises again to maximize profits in order to make the investors happy. Management views the low wages of employees as unimportant in relation to rendering record profits to the investors.

The exclusion of all other interests for the ultimate goal of profit maximization of the firm is ethically wrong, and the company that makes this decision is not being socially responsible. The interests of society and others with relevant relationships to the firm should be considered. The concept of maximum profit should be replaced with the idea of what is a reasonable profit for the firm while taking into consideration that all human interests are relevant and important.

Stakeholder Concept stands for the proposition that others in society have a stake or interest in the making of ethical business decisions in addition to the customary decision-makers of the business firm. The customary decision-makers of a corporation would be the board of directors, officers and shareholders, or for a sole proprietor, the sole owner himself. Nontraditional, non-owner stakeholders could be employees, creditors, suppliers, debtors, customers, local community, society as a whole, and others with similar interests.

This theory is based on the well-being of the stakeholder. Each stakeholder has an individual or societal interest in maintaining and protecting his self-interest. Here, the voices and opinions of the stakeholders should be considered and factored into the ethical decision-making process. There should be some type of equitable and fair system of allocating the appropriate emphasis or weight to assign to the interests of the individual or societal stakeholders.

Two views are presented in the process of decision-making. The first view has the traditional decision-makers, such as the members of a limited liability company, making the final ethical decision. This final decision is made after hearing, considering and evaluating all of the known factors from all of the known stakeholders. The stakeholders provide input into the final ethical decision, but they do not participate in making the decision. Only the good faith of the traditional decision-makers is relied upon. The second view not only allows non-owner stakeholders to provide stakeholder interest and input during the evaluation process along with the traditional corporate areas of concern, but additionally, it permits non-owner stakeholders to cast votes in the actual decision-making procedure. The reasoning is that non-owner stakeholders in reality are surrogate owners of the firm because society itself has an interest that the business make the correct ethical decision, and after all, society is the ultimate authorizing agent for corporate existence.

Under this theory, non-owners of the business, such as creditors, customers, the local community, society as a whole and others with an interest in the firm, termed stakeholders, should have input into the decision-making of the firm. When considering the views of non-owners in making decisions, the firm will be acting in a socially responsible manner.

This is a commendable ethical theory; however, a glaring weakness is that its proper implementation solely depends on the attitude of those in decision-making positions. To what degree will stakeholder interests be considered? Are they as equally important as the interests of the firm? How are these interests allocated?

Another question deals with the issue of stakeholder identification. Who are the stakeholders? Traditionally, stakeholders were recognized to be employees, creditors, suppliers, debtors, customers and others directly dealing with the company. The local community and society were also included. But who comprises the local community, and how far does it extend? Society is a general catch-all term. Does the term society include all of mankind, or is the term more restrictive?

To what extent should stakeholders have a voice in corporate decision-making? Should they be granted a nonbinding vote on the corporate board of directors? Or, should they be granted a binding vote? Or, should they merely be given the right to be heard at board meetings? The questions go on and on. Herein lie the problems of stakeholder interest. The proper consideration of stakeholder interests is a matter of defining what is proper under all the facts and circumstances of the particular business situation. Defining *proper* may be extremely difficult.

Moral Minimum theory stipulates that the ethical duty of the corporation is met so long as the business, while operating at a profit, does not injure anyone or cause
damage to society. While attempting not to, if the business firm does injure someone or causes damage to society, it can still satisfy its ethical responsibility by providing adequate compensation for the injury or by correcting whatever damage it caused.

Here, the *good faith test* is applied to the factual situation. The good faith test requires the business firm at a moral minimum to act with honesty and integrity in making any ethical business decision. In the event someone is injured as a result of a bona fide, good faith business decision, the firm must adequately compensate the victim for the injury. The same concept applies to harm caused to society. For example, suppose a manufacturer of chemicals dispatches a delivery truck to a customer. While en route, the chemical container begins to leak, causing pollution along the highway. The company would meet its moral responsibility to society under the moral minimum theory by properly cleaning up the chemical spill.

Should the firm's operations cause injury or damage, its social responsibility will be met if the injury is compensated or the damage is repaired. The problem here is that the firm may weigh the cost of repairing the damage against the profit desired from causing the damage. If the profit outweighs the cost of repair, the firm could choose this course of action and satisfy its responsibility to society. The firm may deliberately make an unethical decision but subsequently, make it ethical under this theory by repairing the damage. An unethical decision initially made cannot adequately be justified and made ethical by a later corporate act.

Another problem with this concept is the name itself. Can there really be degrees to morality, or is it more accurate to say that acts are either moral or not moral? On that basis, does a moral minimum really exist? For instance, this theory holds that it is ethically proper to lie provided that the lie does not cause injury or damage. However, this would be inconsistent with the natural law since lying violates truth.

Business Citizenship theory holds that a corporation, limited-liability company or other business organization form exists as a business citizen within the social structure. The business exists because society allows it to exist under certain terms and conditions. Like a normal citizen, the business citizen has societal duties and responsibilities which is expected and required of it.

Business citizenship mandates the corporate responsibility of sustaining and improving society. The ordinary business responsibilities, such as paying taxes, fair wages, legal compliance, and so forth, are assumed to be accomplished. According to this theory, the social responsibility of business goes far beyond the ordinary and accepted legal requirements of operating a business. Here, business has the social responsibility to create a better society through a sharing of profits. These private profits are given for public uses and purposes.

As an example, corporate profits should be utilized to subsidize public money for the construction of schools in order to provide better education for children. Further, profits could also be utilized for the purchase of school books and other educational materials. Corporate profits, when added to taxes designated for public education, would presumably create a better education system. The whole burden of public educa-

tion should not be borne
solely by private citizens but by business as well. The reasoning here is that societal citizenship is broadened to include business. Business, like ordinary citizens, should have responsibility for improving society and business
should designate a portion of profits to accomplish this end.
After all, it is society that gives business the authority to operate and make a profit; therefore, business has the social responsibility to contribute a portion of its profits
for the betterment of society. This view advocates that the primary purpose of business creation is for business to share its profits with society. Shareholder interests, investor interests and corporate retained profits are subordinate.

The social responsibility of the business firm as a citizen of society is to do good for society. Society empowers business to exist and prosper; therefore, the ultimate objective of business should be to achieve good. Under the business citizenship theory, business is morally obligated to designate a portion of its profits for the betterment of society and mankind.

The High Road of Corporate Responsibility to Society

The high road of societal corporate responsibility emphatically eliminates both the profit maximization and moral minimum theories for the reasons previously discussed under those topics. This leaves us with two possible acceptable theories: the stakeholder concept and business citizenship. There are ethically desirable characteristics under each theory, and our suggestion is that decision-makers should adhere to these two theories when making ethical decisions. Not that one theory should be considered to the exclusion of the other, but they should be considered together as the factual situations dictate.

Under both theories, business executives, while maintaining vigilance over corporate affairs, look beyond the company interests to other societal concerns. The stakeholder concept considers others, many of whom have direct contact with the firm, such as employees, creditors, debtors, and customers. The local community and society at large may also be considered. The corporate interests, as well as these outside interests, are taken into consideration when making any business decision. The weight to be given these oftentimes competing interests is within the sound discretion of the decision-makers. The business citizenship theory goes further than the stakeholder concept. This *do good theory* fosters the idea of using the structure of the business firm as a tool for the betterment of society in general. A portion of business profits are designated for worthy charitable (churches, hospitals), research (cancer or AIDS), humanitarian (hunger, natural disaster relief), social (education) and other causes. What portion of company profits to set aside for these causes, of course, rests within the judgment of the decision-makers. So, the business citizenship theory could, and oftentimes does, actually go beyond the stakeholder concept in terms of safeguarding and promoting societal concerns. The business citizenship theory presupposes the firm is making a profit and contributing to the chosen causes out of those profits.

The ethical high road to corporate social responsibility could be an appropriate combination of these two theories, where stakeholder interests are properly considered when making corporate decisions along with a return of a fair portion of the corporate profits to society for worthy causes.

Ethical Behavior and Profitability of the Firm

This brings us to the question that addresses the issue of profitability of the ethical business. Ethics is not a deterrent to profit but rather, generally increases the profitability of the firm. All business transactions necessarily have at their core the element of *trustworthiness*.

All parties to the transactions must believe that the others will follow through and do what they promised to do. Trust is the glue that holds capitalism together. When ethics fail, trust fails.

With good ethics, trust flourishes. Any discussion of ethics would be incomplete without including trust.

If business firms did not trust each other, they would not do business with each other. Imagine for a moment a world in which no business honored their contractual obligations. Because of the universal breach of trust, business would grind to a halt, and the court systems could not possibly handle all the cases. Everybody, businesses, employers, employees, customers, suppliers, creditors, debtors and others, would all be suing each other. Ethical behavior builds trust, and trust has a positive impact on the bottom line of the firm for several reasons.

1.   Trust builds confidence.
2.   Trust builds loyalty.
3.   Trust fosters good relations.
4.   Trust solidifies long-term dealings.
5.   Trust reduces the cost of doing business.
6.   Trust promotes societal approval of business.

Trust builds confidence in corporate management that has established a past pattern of ethical behavior. The customer knows he can depend on the product or service. The supplier knows he will be paid. The employee knows he will be treated fairly and equitably. Society can depend on the firm making ethically-correct business decisions.

Trust builds loyalty toward the firm in many ways. Loyalty really is a two-way street that starts at the top, and permeates just about every facet of the business enterprise.

When management is loyal to shareholders, shareholders return the loyalty. When the firm is fair to customers and consistently delivers a quality product or service, customers respond not only by repeat business, but by recommending the firm to others, thereby expanding the customer base. When management demonstrates its loyalty to employees, employees respond likewise. A supplier that received fair treatment over the years will become loyal to the firm. Thus, a consistent demonstration of loyalty provides a sort of reciprocity, or mutual exchange, of loyalty between the firm and everyone who deals with it. Loyalty is the result of an unbroken circle of trust. All parties profit from loyalty. Good business relations are a direct result of a viable trust relationship. Trust promotes openness between the parties. When disputes develop between business and those dealing with business, and we know that disputes are inevitable, an environment of trust will enable the parties to move forward in an effort to resolve their dispute without litigation. Once the dispute is settled, the parties who have had a good trust relationship will have a good opportunity to continue doing business together. Expensive litigation has been avoided, and because no harsh feelings have resulted from the dispute, the firm can continue its profitable relationship.

Trust is ordinarily not established instantly, or even quickly, between parties. It is usually nurtured over time. When trust is established, it sets the stage for long-term dealings between the parties. Each knows they can depend on each other. Long-term dealings enable management to look and plan beyond next quarter or next year. Long-term, effective planning allows the firm to position its resources in order to take maximum advantage of market conditions, thereby enhancing profits.

Trust reduces the cost of doing business. We have already seen that trust decreases the amount of litigation which, even if the firm prevails, can be enormously expensive. When more trust is placed in workers, less management   oversight is needed.   Less management expenses translate into a larger bottom line. Trust and honesty are like brother and sister. Trustworthy employees do not steal from the firm; therefore, theft losses to the firm are minimized. In firms whose nature of business requires teamwork, trust among teams and team members fosters efficiency. More efficiency generally means more profits. In an environment of trust, workers are more productive and happy. Their attitudes are better, and they do their jobs better. This attitude may be passed on to suppliers, customers, and others. Particularly in research and development departments, researchers need a creative setting. Creativeness is encouraged by a trustworthy environment. Employees with strong moral values and religious convictions are more likely to behave honestly and be better workers, which taken together, tends to promote productivity and, in turn, increases the profitability of the firm.

A company with a good reputation for truth and honesty has the unqualified approval of society. This is the type of company that is respected and encouraged by all levels of government and by society in general. An ethical company that honors the terms of its contracts will rarely end up in the court system. An ethical company that respects the environment and adheres to environmental standards will require less governmental regulation and oversight. A company that seeks to treat its employees fairly, pay reasonable salaries and provide adequate benefits will be respected throughout the community and create a ripple-effect within the industry.

Emphatically, the success of capitalism is dependent upon universal trust and the utilization and manifestation of high moral standards, both within the capitalist superstructure, i.e., the entire makeup of business and industry, and the totality of society. When ethics are violated, the rules of capitalism involving honesty and fair play are violated which may give the violator a temporary advantage in the market place. Competitors observe an uneven playing field with some advantage being obtained by a rival business. To level the field of competition, otherwise ethical companies may be tempted to cut corners and engage in ethically questionable activities. As more and more companies abandon their morals, capitalism is compromised and weakened, both ethical and unethical companies may experience downturns in the long run, and society suffers.

A company with a good ethical record for truth, honesty, integrity and fairness forms the basic structure of capitalism.

Here, trust flourishes and permeates not only within the company, but with all whom the company deals. Customer satisfaction is enhanced. Stockholder confidence is strengthened, and the company is lauded as a good corporate citizen.

Examples of Ethical Firms

Now, let's look at some companies that have been very profitable as well as ethical. Each year *Business Ethics, The Magazine of Corporate Responsibility*, publishes a list of the 100 best corporate citizens. The firms eligible for the list come from approximately 1100 companies from the S&P 500, Russell 1000 and the Domini 400 Social Index. Ratings are based on eight stakeholder categories:

1. total return to stockholders;
2. community;
3. governance;
4. diversity;
5. employees;
6. environment;
7. human rights; and
8. product.

The total return to stockholders is based on a three-year average of total return to shareholders which includes stock price appreciation plus dividends. All other scores are based on an analysis of various strengths and concerns companies demonstrate in each stakeholder category. The overall score is calculated by averaging together the scores from each of the eight areas.

The company receiving the number one rating for 2006 was *Green Mountain Coffee Roasters, Inc.* from Vermont. What began as a quaint café in 1981, today has become the nation's leading specialty coffee company. Employing 600, Green Mountain experienced 2005 revenue of $161.5 million with net income of $9 million. This was a 15 percent increase over 2004. Since its founding, the company has been socially and environmentally active. In 1989, it formed an environmental committee and created a rainforest nut coffee to support the Rainforest Alliance, a non-profit organization dedicated to protecting ecosystems. The company has been a pioneer in the fair trade movement which pays coffee growers stable, fair prices and has become active in countries where coffee is grown. Green Mountain has been in the top 10 on the list for the last four years. It was named by *Forbes Magazine* in 2005 as one of the *"200 Best Small Companies in America."* Each year the company contributes at least five percent pre-tax profits to support socially responsible initiatives. Green Mountain is certified as a CERES (Coalition for Environmentally Responsible Economics) company which means that it is committed to acting responsibly toward the environment in its business dealings.

Hewlett-Packard Company was number two on the 2006 Best Corporate Citizens list. Since the inception of the 100 Best Corporate Citizens seven years ago, Hewlett-Packard is the only company that has made the top ten listing each year. This 151,000-employee firm had sales in 2005 of $86.7 billion with a one-year sales growth of 8.5 percent. It had a one-year net income sales growth of 31.4 percent with a net income of $2.4 billion. The 2005 employee growth rate was 6.3 percent. Hewlett-Packard manufactures and markets a full range of high-tech equipment to enterprise and consumer customers.   Community service and diversity are the most important corporate citizenship issues. The company has a vice president of global inclusion and diversity that networks with company managers around the world to deal with workforce diversity and disabled employees. In 2000, Hewlett-Packard created the Digital Village, which established computer centers in small villages in Latin America, Asia and Africa. Environmentally, the company has reduced greenhouse gas emissions by controlling employee travel, using renewable energy and recycling.

Timberland Company has been on the 100 Best Corporate Citizens list in *Business Ethics Magazine* for the seventh consecutive year. In 2006, it is listed number six. *Timberland* is best known for manufacturing and marketing footwear. In 2005, it had a net income of $164 million on sales of $1.6 billion. The company has 5,600 employees. Its 2005 net income growth increased 7.8 percent over 2004. Through its *Path of Service*, Timberland has become a strong promoter of employee volunteers. This program allows employees to devote 40 hours of company-compensated time each year to community service during regular working hours. In an effort to reduce its environmental impact, Timberland has increased its use of renewable energy and resources. To increase the awareness of the crisis of genocide in the Sudan and to inspire civil and political action, the company is creating a limited edition "Save Darfur" boot. Timberland is also introducing a line of products made of organic and all natural fibers.

The Natural Law, Ten Commandments and Corporate Profitability

In Chapter Two, we suggested that the Judeo-Christian tradition in the United States defines "natural law" as the precepts that can be found in the second tablet of the Ten Commandments. Consisting of the insights of human conduct and behavior that our Creator has made inherent in our nature, the natural law gives mankind a reference system that really works. Natural law offers order to a chaotic world and certainty in place of futility.

The cases of Green Mountain, Hewlett-Packard, and Timberland demonstrate evidence that their leaders respect the natural law in their corporate dealings. For instance, the natural law indicates that stealing is wrong and yet we saw in

Enron, WorldCom and Tyco rampant theft of corporate resources. Yet in Green Mountain, Hewlett-Packard and Timberland we observe a commitment to honesty and integrity. While it is true that a company doesn't proclaim, "We are honest, and we do not steal," the character of the company is demonstrated through   commitment to stakeholder interests as a good corporate citizen. The attitude respecting property ownership permeates the firm. This was not true at Tyco. The $2.1 million birthday party that former Tyco CEO, Dennis Kozlowski, gave for his wife was an outright theft of company funds which others in the company observed. Not only did Kozlowski commit numerous thefts, but his subordinates followed his lead and did also. In successful firms, being honest is profitable as is clearly demonstrated not only by the income statements of Green Mountain, Hewlett-Packard and Timberland, but also by the successful financial performance of the other 97 companies listed on the 100 best corporate citizens list, as well as innumerable other ethically successful firms doing business throughout the world.

One can easily see that the colossal failures of Enron, WorldCom and Tyco were the result of a multitude of lies and deceptions. We have previously seen that truth not only goes to the core of human existence but also to the essence of business existence. Any company committed to the interests of stakeholders is also committed to truth. These two commitments go hand in hand.

The natural law speaks out against covetousness. To covet means to possess an inordinate desire to have what belongs to another. When this desire becomes unregulated and excessive, scheming and planning occur to obtain that which is coveted. An example of extreme covetousness is illustrated by the uncontrolled desire of former WorldCom CEO, Bernie Ebbers, to own tens of thousands of acres of land. This culpable desire led him to obtain enormous personal loans from WorldCom to purchase the land. In effect, he was using the shareholders' equity as his personal bank.

The natural law and Ten Commandments encourage an over-arching theme of stewardship toward fellow man and the environment. Green Mountain responds to this theme through its contribution of at least five percent of its pre-tax profits to socially responsible initiatives. It is a CERES company dedicated to protecting ecosystems and acting responsibly toward the environment. Hewlett-Packard is a world leader in promoting diversity in the workplace and has created computer learning centers in many third-world countries. It is also committed to using renewable energy and has taken extensive measures to promote recycling. Likewise, Timberland is a strong advocate of stewardship through its Path of Service that promotes employee volunteerism at company expense. The company has also increased its use of renewable energy and resources in a concerted effort to be more environmentally friendly. It is pro-active in increasing public awareness of the genocide crisis in the Sudan.

These three companies and the other 97 in the Top *100 Best Corporate Citizens* (Table 5.1) are just a small sampling of the many companies that are committed to ethical behavior and have affirmative programs which demonstrate their commitment to stakeholder interests. These programs, with their emphasis on stakeholder interests, are really extensions of the natural law. Companies that make a conscious effort to follow the natural law reduce the number of occasions in which ethical slip-ups occur. All of the companies found in the *100 Best Corporate Citizens* have been tremendously successful and profitable. Adherence to the natural law makes good ethical sense as well as dollars and cents. Indeed, following the natural law is profitable!

Summary

1.   Unethical business behavior may be very costly and unprofitable.

2. Businesses have a responsibility to society that may be expressed in one or more of the following theories – profit maximization, stakeholder concept, moral minimum and business citizenship.

3. Ethically desirable characteristics are present in the stakeholder concept and business citizenship theories of corporate responsibility and are recommended as the preferred approaches to achieve socially-responsible corporate behavior.

4. Trust is the glue that holds capitalism together, and without trust, business cannot be successful.

5. The natural law is a characterization of good and provides business with an outstanding reference system for ethical conduct.

6. The top 100 businesses listed in *Business Ethics, The Magazine of Corporate Responsibility*, are noted for achieving both high ethical standards and strong corporate profitability.

Table 4-1
Business Ethics 100 Best Corporate Citizens 2006

Rank	Company	Rank	Company
1	Green Mountain Coffee Roasters, Inc.	27	UnionBanCal Corporation.
2	Hewlett-Packard Company	28	Wild Oats Markets, Inc.
3	Advanced Micro Devices, Inc.	29	American Express Company
4	Motorola, Inc.	30	Northwest Natural Gas Company
5	Agilent Technologies, Inc.	31	Coherent, Inc.
6	Timberland Company (The)	32	Gaiam, Inc.
7	Salesforce.com, Inc.	33	Eastman Kodak Company
8	Cisco Systems, Inc.	34	Sovereign Bancorp, Inc.
9	Dell Inc.	35	Applied Materials, Inc.
10	Texas Instruments Incorporated	36	Nationwide Financial Services, Inc.
11	Intel Corporation	37	Heartland Financial USA, Inc.
12	Johnson & Johnson	38	Freddie Mac
13	NIKE, Inc.	39	Synovus Financial Corp.
14	General Mills Incorporated	40	Chicago Mercantile Exchange Holdings Inc.
15	Pitney Bowes, Inc.	41	International Business Machines Corporation
16	Wells Fargo & Company	42	Adobe Systems Incorporated
17	Starbucks Corporation	43	3M Company
18	Wainwright Bank & Trust Company	44	First Horizon National Corporation
19	St. Paul Travelers Companies, Inc. (The)	45	Office Depot, Inc.
20	Ecolab Inc.	46	SLM Corporation
21	Gap, Inc. (The)	47	Whole Foods Market, Inc.
22	Herman Miller, Inc.	48	United Parcel Service, Inc.
23	Southwest Airlines Co.	49	Whirlpool Corporation
24	Interface, Inc.	50	United Natural Foods, Inc.
25	Apple Computer, Inc.	51	State Street Corporation
26	Chittenden Corporation	52	Student Loan Corporation

Table 4-1 continued
Business Ethics 100 Best Corporate Citizens 2006

Rank	Company	Rank	Company
53	Total System Services, Inc.	77	Nordstrom, Inc.
54	Tennant Company	78	Lam Research Corporation
55	Kellogg Company	79	KeyCorp
56	Cathay General Bancorp, Inc.	80	Akamai Technologies, Inc.
57	McGraw-Hill Companies, Inc.	81	Symantec Corporation
58	Zimmer Holdings, Inc.	82	Micron Technology, Inc.
59	Modine Manufacturing Company	83	East West Bancorp, Inc.
60	Northern Trust Corporation	84	PepsiCo, Inc.
61	Cummins, Inc.	85	Graco, Inc.
62	Citigroup Inc.	86	Autodesk, Inc.
63	Moina Healthcare, Inc.	87	Timken Company, (The)
64	Nature's Sunshine Products, Inc.	88	American Tower Corporation
65	Washington Post Company	89	Hartford Financial Services Group (The)
66	Darden Restaurants, Inc.	90	Procter & Gamble Company
67	Biomet, Inc.	91	Xilinx, Inc.
68	Bank of Hawaii Corporation	92	Air Products & Chemicals, Inc.
69	Brady Corporation	93	Grainger (W.W.), Inc.
70	Sun Microsystems, Inc.	94	Gen-Probe Incorporated
71	WGL Holdings, Inc.	95	Baldor Electric Company
72	Ambac Financial Group, Inc.	96	BB&T Corporation
73	Johnson Controls, Inc.	97	Principal Financial Group, Inc.
74	Bright Horizons Family Solutions, Inc.	98	Apogee Enterprises, Inc.
75	Becton Dickinson and Company	99	IDEXX Laboratories, Inc.
76	Genentech, Inc.	100	Rockwell Collins

Source: *Business Ethics, The Magazine of Corporate Responsibility*, Spring 2006

5

The Law as an Ethical Threshold

The *law* has a truly panoramic character. Over the years, laws have been made by mankind for the benefit, control and governance of fellow human beings and the innumerable activities of human existence. It seems that the law has always been with us, from the earliest civilizations to the present. We cannot escape it. We may climb to the top of Mount Everest, the highest spot on Earth at an elevation of 29,055 feet, and we are still subject to the law. We can travel to the middle of the Pacific Ocean, the North Pole, or anywhere else, but we always have the law with us. Even if we travel in space, there is a new area of law termed *Space Law* to govern our activities there!

Laws have been created to define what conduct is *right* or *wrong* for the people within whatever societal framework they live. Prehistoric societies governed themselves by *customary laws* that were based on customs and general usage in the community. The invention of the written word enabled the law to be recorded and assembled in *law codes*, making the law available to the masses. As a result, laws have enabled societies to function more effectively and people to live more peaceful lives.

Ethics and the Law

The natural law has had an incredibly large influence on the moral content of the laws that mankind has enacted over the years. Because the natural law always rings true, its precepts have informed legislatures and courts as laws are developed, written and tested. And, because many leaders in our nation's history have embraced a Judeo-Christian perspective, the Ten Commandments have been frequently used as the definitive expression of the natural law.

As we discussed in chapter two, the natural law does not change over time. Theft, lying and murder have always been wrong. The natural law is timeless. However, unlike ethics, society's laws do change over time as the needs and desires of society change. For example, the national need for environmental protection prompted the United States Congress in 1969 to pass the National Environmental Policy Act (NEPA). Oftentimes, although society does not actually need a change in the law, the desires of society become so strong and widespread that the lawmakers respond to the desire and change the law. For example, some states have passed legislation legalizing the personal possession of small amounts of marijuana. As time marches on, so does the advance of technology, and the law changes to accommodate these advances. For example, in 1900, there was no law relating to aviation. As aviation technology developed and progressed, laws were written to reflect these changes. Today, aviation law is a huge body of jurisprudence.

The law sets the minimum, or the bottom floor, for all ethical conduct. When one disobeys the law, not only is the law broken, but the disobedience is a violation of ethics. When one breaks the law, one acts unethically. Thus, as shown in Figure 5-1, we see that the one act of stealing is both a violation of law and a violation of ethics. However, the sanctions or punishments for these two violations are quite different (Figure 5-2). Theft has criminal, as well as civil, legal sanctions. The criminal law divides theft into two categories: petit larceny (i.e., the value of item stolen is under $500) and grand larceny (i.e., the value of the item stolen is over $500). Petit larceny is a misdemeanor crime, and the punishment includes a small fine and imprisonment of up to one year. Grand larceny, on the other hand, is a felony whose punishment includes a large fine, imprisonment of more than one year, and in some cases, loss of the right to vote plus a perpetual prohibition against the possession of a firearm.

Figure 5-1

Violation of Law and Ethics

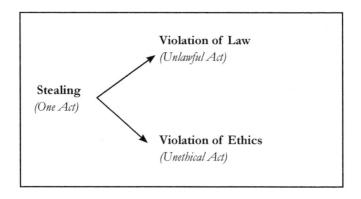

Figure 5-2

Sanctions for Legal (Criminal and Civil) and Ethical Violations

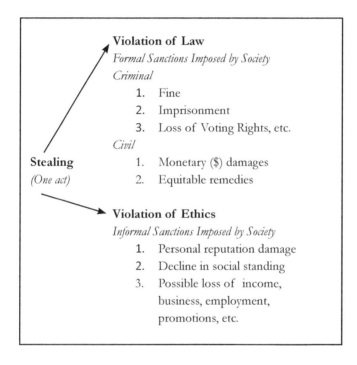

Stealing
(One act)

Violation of Law
Formal Sanctions Imposed by Society
Criminal
　　1.　Fine
　　2.　Imprisonment
　　3.　Loss of Voting Rights, etc.
Civil
　　1.　Monetary ($) damages
　　2.　Equitable remedies

Violation of Ethics
Informal Sanctions Imposed by Society
　　1.　Personal reputation damage
　　2.　Decline in social standing
　　3.　Possible loss of income,
　　　　business, employment,
　　　　promotions, etc.

The civil legal sanction subjects the law breaker to a lawsuit brought by the victim of the larceny for the recovery of monetary compensation based on the value of the item(s) stolen, other incidental damages suffered as a result of the larceny and possibly other equitable remedies, such as injunction.

Additionally, the unethical conduct of stealing may subject the perpetrator to informal ethical sanctions imposed by society. These sanctions may include damage to or loss of reputation in the community, a decline in business if engaged in business, loss of employment or promotions, loss of business and social opportunities, damage to and/or loss of social standing in the community, damage to and/or loss of friendships and social relationships and others.

While we have seen that the law represents the ethical minimum for society, many situations occur where the criminal law is not violated but where the civil law is violated. The conduct is still unethical. Such is the case of lying. Lying, like stealing, is a violation against the natural law. Under certain circumstances, lying can be a criminal offense, such as perjury or telling an untruth to the Federal Bureau of Investigation.

But, let's take the case where a lie is told in a business context which is not a criminal act in and of itself. Assume that Alfred and Ben enter into a valid contract wherein Alfred promises to manufacture 10 laptop computers according to certain specifications for delivery to Ben's place of business on a certain date. Ben agrees and promises to pay a designated price per computer within 30 days of delivery, yet Ben knows that his business is on the brink of bankruptcy and that he will not have assets to pay for the computers. Alfred complies with his part of the agreement, manufactures the computers and delivers them by the contract date. Ben accepts delivery of the computers knowing that he cannot possibly pay for them due to the financial condition of his company and immediately ships them to Timbuktu to a buyer who pays him cash. Ben takes the cash and averts bankruptcy but refuses to pay Alfred the purchase price.

By not fulfilling his part of the contract to remit the agreed upon purchase price for the computers, Ben has violated not only the civil law of contracts, but also the ethical prohibition against lying and deceptive behavior. He has subjected himself to a civil lawsuit as well as the other informal sanctions which may be imposed by society for his unethical act (see Figure 5-3).

Figure 5-3

Sanctions for Legal (Civil) and Ethical Violations

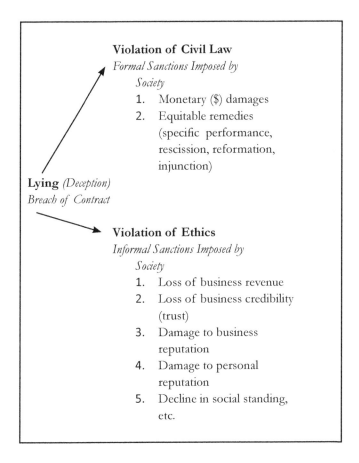

Oftentimes in the course of human events, unethical acts occur which are unethical by themselves but carry no formal societal punishments. The act is unethical but does not violate either the criminal or civil law. Such is the case of the lie when the lie does not involve the breaking of the law (see Figure 5-4).

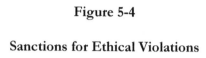

Figure 5-4

Sanctions for Ethical Violations

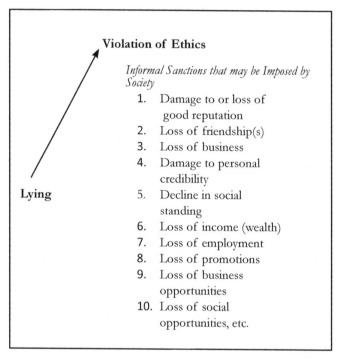

Telling a lie violates the Ten Commandments' prohibition against bearing false witness. Let's assume that Joe tells his friend, Andy, an untruth about the ownership of a certain vehicle. Joe tells Andy that he owns a vintage 1925 Rolls Royce automobile when he does not own it. Joe is seeking to enhance his standing with Andy who is an antique vehicle collector. Andy finds out about the lie. Joe not only may suffer personally from loss of status as an honest person but also some of the other informal, societal sanctions listed in Figure 5.4. Additionally, Joe may feel the pain of his conscience for the lie and suffer some type of emotional distress.

Good Law and Bad Law

All *good law* should be obeyed because it is legally and ethically correct to do so. A good law is defined as a man-made law which respects the natural law. Society should obey good law even though there may be a disagreement about the purpose or wisdom of the law, for example, the federal and state laws which require us to pay income taxes. As taxpayers, we may not agree with the tax laws and how the government spends collected tax revenues, but we still should obey. We have a democratic form of government in which we elect representatives, senators and others to represent the people in the halls of government. These people make laws to govern us. One area of governance deals with financing governmental operations through taxation. The duly elected representatives of the people have made these laws on taxation which do not conflict with the natural law; therefore, these laws, although there may be some disagreement on the wisdom of their passage, are termed good laws and should be obeyed.

A *bad law* may be disobeyed because it is ethically correct to do so. A bad law is defined as a law that violates the natural law. An example of bad law is illustrated by what happened in Germany in the 1930's. Adolf Hitler, the Nazi dictator who came to power in 1933, blamed the Jewish people for Germany's economic depression and began a vicious and inhuman campaign against them. The German government passed laws which stripped Jews of their citizenship, permitted governmental seizure of Jewish property and destruction of synagogues and forced thousands into concentration camps. After the beginning of World War II in 1939, Hitler, utilizing governmental authority, ordered millions of Jews executed in the mass murders during what came to be called the *Holocaust*. What happened in Germany was the *worst of bad law*. It violated the natural law. It makes no difference that the German Parliament passed laws sanctioning these atrocities to take place; the laws were manifestly illegal and immoral because they violated the natural law. Ethically, these bad laws *should* and *must* be disobeyed.

Laws Regulating Business

History has revealed that if unregulated by government, some individuals will utilize their superior economic and political power to take advantage of those in weaker socioeconomic standings. An analysis of the industrial revolution of the late 1800's in the United States demonstrates this point. The super rich and politically powerful robber barons of that period conspired together and created huge monopolies which allowed them to capture immense markets which, in turn, permitted them to charge high and noncompetitive prices. The economically weak were exploited by the economically powerful. These so-called robber barons, who were very, very few in number, became incredibly rich while the masses languished in poverty. Children were utilized as a cheap labor source. Dangerous and unhealthy working conditions were commonplace. Workers were viewed by big business as merely expendable objects to be paid as little as possible, overworked and, if injured or disabled, discarded.

The exploitation of labor existed for several decades, but the public outcry against the monopoly owners for their outrageous and unconscionable acts against labor   became so intense and widespread that American workers eventually were granted greater protections and rights under law. The leaders in government finally recognized that some regulation was necessary to protect the rights and well-being of the weaker members of society. Also, government   officials eventually realized that reasonable
regulation is essential for the creation of an ideal business environment. As a consequence, a number of laws regulating business have been passed that not only protect consumers, employees and the environment, but also seek to ensure ethi-

cal conduct and decision-making. Let us review some of these laws.

Laws Protecting Consumers

Until about the middle of the twentieth century, buyers of goods and services in the United States were subject to the legal doctrine of *caveat emptor* or *let the buyer beware.* Consumers essentially purchased at their own risk. The legal theory was that there was little or no recourse against the seller if the consumer purchased a defective good or service because the consumer should have inspected or checked out the good or service before purchase. Caveat emptor heavily favored business. However, today the rule has shifted to become *caveat venditor*, or *let the seller beware.* Consumer protection laws are directed toward fair treatment and the protection of consumers from the misconduct of merchants and others.

A large number of federal and state laws and regulations have been enacted to protect consumers who buy goods and services. A partial listing of areas of consumer protection is found in Table 5-1.

Laws Protecting Employees

Prior to the Industrial Revolution, *laissez-faire* (government hands-off) was the doctrine that defined the employer-employee relationship. Because of the generally one-on-one relationship, employers and employees had approximately equal bargaining power.

Table 5-1

Areas of Consumer Protection

Advertising	Debt Collection
Bait and Switch	Door-to-Door Sales
Consumer Contracts	Franchises
Consumer Leasing	Product Labeling
Credit Cards	Product Safety
Credit Opportunity	Product Warranties
and Billing	Real estate sales
Credit Reputation	Seals of Approval
Protection	Truth-in Lending

However, when the country became industrialized in the late 1800's, the employment relationship radically changed. Employers, many of whom had become large corporations, became much more powerful at the bargaining table, and individual employees lost much of their ability to effectively bargain for their interests. Thus, a great disparity developed between labor and management. To further worsen the plight of labor, many employers extensively utilized child labor, working conditions were often unsafe, working hours were long and wages were extremely low. The federal congress, as well as state legislatures, recognized these problems, and a number of statutes were enacted to protect the rights of workers. Labor unions were made lawful, and collective bargaining enabled employees to be better represented at labor-management negotiations.

A number of laws have been passed to protect employees. Some of the more important protective areas are listed in Table 5-2, on the next page.

Table 5-2

Employee Protection Laws

Affirmative action	Private pension funds
Age discrimination	Racial discrimination
Child labor	Sex discrimination
Civil rights	Social Security
Collective bargaining	State labor laws
Equal pay	Unemployment
Federal labor laws	compensation
Immigration employment	Union legalization
Insurance	Worker disability
Minimum wage and	Worker safety & health
Overtime	Workers' compensation

Laws Protecting the Environment

During the normal course of living, manufacturing and consuming, people and business enterprises produce water, air and noise pollution, and hazardous wastes that damage the environment and potentially injure or kill human beings and other living things. Environmental laws have existed since the Middle Ages in one form or another. In the United States until the 1950's, the common law provided a forum wherein polluters could be sued to recover damages. The equitable remedy of injunction was also available.

However, as our country became more urbanized and complicated with competing societal interests, the federal and state governments realized that comprehensive environmental legislation was needed to safeguard the environment and protect the population against unsafe pollution. Since the passage of the Federal Air Pollution Control Act of 1955, numerous federal and state laws have been passed to protect the environment against pollution and to regulate hazardous and toxic substances. Many of these statutes provide both civil and criminal penalties. The major subject areas of environmental protection are summarized in Table 5-3.

Table 5-3

Environmental Protection Subject Areas

Air pollution	Oil spills
Endangered species	Pesticides
Fungicides	State laws
Hazardous substances	Superfund (cleanup)
Insecticides	Thermal pollution
Noise pollution	Toxic substances
Nuclear waste	Water pollution
Ocean dumping	Wetlands

Many corporations have recognized the importance of safeguarding the environment by adopting what is commonly referred to as *The Valdez Principles* (Table 5-4). Formed in 1989, the *Coalition for Environmentally Responsible Economics (CERES)*, formulated this set of ten corporate commitments to provide a framework for corporations relating to their societal responsibility to protect and enhance the world environment.

Corporate adherence to these principles is totally voluntary and carries absolutely no force of law. These principles represent a positive business attitude toward environmental protection and clearly demonstrate excellent ethical behavior that goes far beyond that of non-adopting businesses.

Table 5-4

The Valdez Principles

1. *Protection of the Biosphere* – minimize pollution

2. *Sustainable Use of Natural Resources* – sustainable use of renewable resources and conserve non-renewable resources

3. *Reduction and Disposal of Waste* – minimize waste and proper waste disposal

4. *Wise Use of Energy* – improve energy efficiency

5. *Risk Reduction* – minimize health and safety risk

6. *Marketing of Safe Products and Services* – insure safe products and services

7. *Damage Compensation* – environmental damage responsibility

8. *Disclosure* – full disclosure of environmental, health and safety hazards

9. *Environmental Directors and Managers* – one board member to represent environmental interests

10. *Assessment and Annual Audit* – public, annual audit.

Laws Promoting Ethical Conduct

Like laws protecting consumers, employees and the environment, laws promoting ethical conduct are numerous. Many laws in this area deal with prohibitions. Some put affirmative duties on individuals and corporations. Ethical misconduct is often difficult to specifically define as a law. For example, it is difficult, if not impossible, to pass a law that makes deception in all business circumstances unlawful. No law can ensure ethical conduct, but some laws, termed watch dog laws, attempt to encourage ethical behavior by some form of governmental monitoring or by mandatory placement of corporate responsibility on certain specified individuals who occupy positions of trust.

The most recent comprehensive law relating to ethical behavior is the Sarbanes-Oxley Act of 2002 (SOX). This act was the result of the public outrage brought about by the financial reporting scandals involving WorldCom, Enron, Xerox, Tyco and others. SOX sought to make corrective changes in the financial reporting systems of publicly traded corporations in an effort to prevent a repeat of the past financial collapses of major United States corporations and to restore public confidence in the stock market. SOX applies to all publicly traded corporations and provides numerous new methods these corporations use to prepare their financial statements. One significant section of SOX requires chief executive officers and chief financial officers of public corporations to personally certify the accuracy of the financial statements of the company. These financial statements must be filed with the Securities and Exchange Commission. SOX correctly places the responsibility on corporate officers and directors to utilize due diligence in taking all necessary and reasonable efforts to ensure that the financial statements of the corporation are complete and accurate. Violations of SOX call for up to $25 million in fines for corporations and up to $5 million in fines and 20 years in prison for individuals violating the law.

Section 307 of SOX mandates that the Securities and Exchange Commission prescribe minimum standards of professional conduct for attorneys representing publicly held companies who practice before the SEC. This section places the burden on attorneys to report any evidence of material violations of securities laws to the corporate general counsel, the board of directors, the chief executive office, or corporate audit committee. SOX also contains enhanced corporate disclosure provisions, auditor provisions, accounting-related provisions and enforcement sections. It is predicted that SOX will be further expanded and refined as needed.

Table 5-5 presents a partial listing of regulations or laws
designed to promote ethical conduct.

Table 5-5

Laws Requiring Ethical Conduct

Federal Sentencing Guidelines Act
Foreign Corrupt Practices Act – bribery for corrupt
   purposes
Market Reform Act of 1990 – market volatility; large
   traders identification
Private Securities Litigation Reform Act of 1995 – private
   securities litigation Professional Associations
Codes of Ethics – Attorneys, accountants, etc.
Racketeer Influenced and Corrupt Organizations Act –
   racketeering investments
Remedies Act of 1990 – to reduce fraudulent financial
   reporting
Sarbanes – Oxley Act of 2002 – Corporate executive
   accountability
Securities Act of 1933 – original distribution of
   securities by issuing corporation
Securities Acts Amendments of 1990 – international fraud
   enforcement
Securities Exchange Act of 1934 – secondary distribution
   of securities
State blue sky laws – to prevent sale of speculative
   schemes with no value
State bribery laws – bribery for corrupt purposes

Summary

1. Law is the threshold for all ethical conduct. If one violates the law, that disobedience is also a violation of ethics.

2. The natural law provides the foundation of all law and ethics. Our nation's Judeo-Christian heritage looks to the second tablet of the Ten Commandments as an effective distillation of the natural law.

3. No individual, business or society will err if the natural law is strictly followed.

4. Good law is to be obeyed; bad law should not be obeyed because it is a violation of natural law.

5. Sanctions are different for violations of law and violations of ethics.

6. Numerous laws protect consumers, employees, the environment and investors.

6

Developing an Ethical Business Organization

Professional golfer Wendy Ward has won four times on the LPGA and made more than $3 million in her career, but perhaps she is best known for the way she lost the 2000 LPGA championship. On the 13th hole, Ward called a one-stroke penalty on herself when, after she had already taken a stance over an 8-foot par putt and grounded her putter, the ball moved slightly. Even though Ward never touched the ball, and even though the ball's movement was so slight that nobody would have noticed had she gone through with the putt, the penalty stroke proved to be the margin between her and winner Juli Inkster.

Professional golf has witnessed many wonderful stories of truth, honor, and square shooting in which competitors have called penalties on themselves for rule infractions that no one else would ever have observed. Bobby Jones, Tom Watson, and Jack Nicklaus are among the golfing greats who have placed honesty and integrity above winning. The actions of these champions give us the inspiration and confidence that winners can and should have ethical integrity. But, how does this come about? As a business leader, how can you develop an organization in which every employee proactively follows high ethical standards? How can you establish an ethical culture in which employees make the right choice whether or not they think someone will catch them if they make the unethical choice? A company must have an effective ethics compliance program to ensure that all understand its values and support policies and codes of conduct that create its ethical environment. In this chapter, we examine some great ideas that business leaders may implement to help make good ethical decision-making second nature to their employees.

Ten Steps to Developing an Ethical Organization

An ethical organization does not happen by chance, and the adoption of codes of ethics, by itself, has not been an effective strategy. Rather, ethical organizations are the result of a conscious and continuous effort on the part of leaders to establish and maintain a full program of ethical compliance. While some corporations have implemented ethics programs that are little more than window dressing, ostensibly to deflect attention and culpability resulting from illegal actions, these approaches ultimately serve no one. Rather, the serious organization should follow ten definitive steps to developing an ethical organization, as these actions provide an excellent underlying structure that can be adapted to meet the needs of various sizes and types of organizations. All are necessary to establish and maintain a high ethical climate and reduce the number of incidents of ethical malfeasance. These actions are summarized in Table 6-1 and discussed in the following section.

Table 6-1

Ten Steps to Develop an Ethical Organization

Action	Description
1. Conduct a Rigorous Self Assessment	Identify company values, shortcomings, and elements of an ethics program already in place. Identify priority areas where there is greater risk that ethical violations may occur within the organization.
2. Hire Ethical Employees	Ensure that new hires have high moral character and sound ethical preparation.
3. Distribute a Written Code of Ethics	Establish clear compliance standards and procedures for all employees, and make these standards readily available.
4. Ensure Commitment from the Top of the Organization	Give responsibility for overseeing compliance to specific high-level personnel. Make commitment part of the compensation package. Ensure that senior management demonstrates its dedication to the program.
5. Ensure All Employees Have Training	Provide timely training that helps employees know rules and values. Build employee capacity to exercise moral judgment.

Table 6-1 continued

Ten Steps to Develop an Ethical Organization

6. Provide Consistent Communication	Provide correspondence and reference materials that explain the requirements. Identify what must be repeated over and over for effectiveness. Use multiple channels to reinforce message.
7. Provide Confidential Resources	Provide confidential resources where employees can go with problems and concerns. Make sure these resources are reliable and trusted.
8. Respond and Enforce Consistently, Promptly and Fairly	Determine how violations will be investigated, violators will be sanctioned and appeals will be conducted. Ensure that processes work smoothly and efficiently, and that roles and responsibilities are clear and well documented.
9. Auditing, Monitoring and Reporting	Determine how program success is to be measured. Include monitoring and assessment to make sure that requirements are being met and employees receive feedback.
10. Make Continuous Improvements	When violations are detected, the organization must take steps to respond to and to prevent further violations.

Adapted from Verschoor (2003)

Step 1: Conduct a Rigorous Self Assessment. A company must understand its own values, shortcomings, the special nature of its business, and its organization structure in determining how to construct an effective ethical compliance program. Accordingly, a necessary prerequisite for any organization beginning to undertake a program is the conduct of a self-assessment survey. As a result of the assessment, business leaders should have a better understanding of what elements of the existing ethical compliance program (if any) can be retained and what needs to be created anew. The self assessment should also identify priority areas where there is greater risk that ethical violations may occur within the organization. For instance, if the firm is frequently involved in securing contracts in foreign countries, perhaps bribery or other violations of the Foreign Corrupt Practices Act should be identified as a priority area. The self-assessment process should provide ample opportunity for every employee to participate and identify their perceptions of the current ethical climate of the organization.

Step 2: Hire Ethical Employees. Naturally, an organization must start with employees that have a well-developed sense of ethics and a strong moral compass. If you begin with an organization full of liars, cheats and scoundrels, you have a very difficult task ahead in creating an ethical organization. The character and level of moral development of prospective employees should be assessed during the interview process, and only those prospects who demonstrate high moral character should be considered for hire.

Step 3: Distribute a Written Code of Ethics. The third step is to establish clear compliance standards and procedures for all employees, and make these standards readily available. Firms have called these standards by three names: (1) codes of conduct, (2) codes of ethics, and (3) statements of values. However, we prefer to draw distinctions, as follows: a code of ethics consists of ethical principles and a set of procedures for reporting violations; a code of conduct specifies ethical and unethical forms of behavior; and a statement of values summarizes the guiding principles of the organization in a format that is primarily intended for communication to stakeholders. Organizations are encouraged to address all three roles in the development of their ethical standards. The standards should also be developed to meet four objectives. First, they should communicate to all those associated with the organization that the purpose of the standards are not just to avoid prosecution or to improve profitability, but rather to promote good ethical behavior of those individuals within the company and the behavior of the organization as a whole. Second, they should be more than a simple catalog of offenses and punishments, but should provide overall direction, guidance and encouragement to promote ethical behavior. Third, they should be constructed in a fashion that ensures broad agreement across the organization as to content. Fourth, they should be constructed of clear and unambiguous language that can be understood by all concerned.

Hewlett-Packard is one firm that has established a reputation for high ethical standards and an effective ethical compliance program. Their Code of Ethics is presented on the company's Website for all to see, and consists of a one-page statement that summarizes ethical values, practices, commitments, relationships and principles (Table 6-2). Leaders that are beginning to develop ethical standards for their respective organization would do well to search the Web and find examples of ethical standards that are used by other organizations. Picking and choosing portions of what other business

Table 6-2
Code of Business Ethics at Hewlett-Packard

At HP we are guided by enduring values that stretch back to our roots — values that reflect basic, fundamental ideas about who we are. Ideas like these:

- there is no substitute for personal and professional integrity;
- doing well and doing good can go hand in hand; and
- trust and respect have always been the cornerstones of our success.

The open doors to our offices reflect the ethical, transparent business practices at every level of the company. They also help foster the open communication that fuels our creativity and camaraderie. We strive to be a company that manages by inspiration, not fear; by sharing information, not guarding it; by empowering people to make decisions; and by unleashing people's talents for the common good.

We are committed to uncompromising integrity.

As a business we must remain profitable to remain viable. But profitable operations are not our only concern. At HP we seek uncompromising integrity through what each individual can contribute — to our customers, our co-workers, our company and our communities.

Table 6-2 continued

Our business success is dependant on trusting relationships. Our reputation is founded on the personal integrity of the company's personnel and our dedication to our principles of:

- **Honesty** in communicating within the company and with our business partners, suppliers and customers, while at the same time protecting the company's confidential information and trade secrets

- **Excellence** in our products and services, by striving to provide high-quality products and services to our customers

- **Responsibility** for our words and actions

- **Compassion** in our relationships with our employees and the communities affected by our business

- **Citizenship** in our observance of all the laws of any country in which we do business, respect for environmental concerns and our service to the community by improving and enriching community life.

- **Fairness** to our fellow employees, stakeholders, business partners, customers and suppliers through adherence to all applicable laws, regulations and policies, and a high standard of behavior.

- **Respect** for our fellow employees, stakeholders, business partners, customers and suppliers while showing willingness to solicit their opinions and value their feedback.

Source: Hewlett-Packard Website

leaders have done is a great way to begin developing standards for your organization.

Standards should reflect upper management's desire for uniform compliance with the values, rules and polices that a firm adopts. Incorporation of the Ten Commandments and natural law as the essential basis of the standard is entirely appropriate. H-P and others have readily incorporated values such as honesty, excellence, personal responsibility and commitment, compassion, citizenship, respect for others and their property, and fairness – all modeled from principles drawn from the Ten Commandments.

Merely having standards is not enough. A company must make the standards understood, and ensure their proper dissemination throughout the organization. Remember that standards do not resolve every possible issue that will be encountered in daily operations, but they do help employees resolve ethical dilemmas by prescribing or limiting certain activities. Standards should communicate what is expected of employees and prescribe penalties should employees violate the code.

Step 4: Ensure Commitment from the Top. The fourth step in creating an ethical compliance program is to obtain commitment from all levels of the organization, especially at the top. A positive ethical climate is necessary or compliance will be seen as "one more job task" rather than as a way of life. If the top of the organization merely gives lip service to the program, employees will view the plan as unimportant and burdensome. Accordingly, the CEO must be seen as an uncompromising proponent of good ethical behavior and a champion of ethical compliance.

The responsibility for overseeing the ethical compliance program should be entrusted to a specific high-level executive with high personal ethical standards, good   intentions   and participatory   leadership   styles.
Responsibility must be matched with authority, however, and there is a tendency to over-restrict the delegation of authority

for fear of exposure. The ethics compliance officer and the ethics oversight committee should be mentors and coaches, not autocrats or dictators. Micromanagement and commands issued "on-high" can create the wrong kind of ethical environment, so that employees act to avoid sanctions rather than act with good ethical reasoning. Management discussions and announcements should support an organization culture that infuses these positions with moral legitimacy.

Real commitment by all employees in each respective area of the organization should be made a part of the executive compensation package for all executives. Furthermore, job descriptions should include moral language that inspires those who serve to identify potential ethical problems and to achieve ethical outcomes consistent with the values of the organization.

Step 5: Ensure All Employees Have Training. Once standards and a compliance officer are in place, the next step is to provide training that educates employees regarding rules and organization values, and builds employee capacity to exercise moral judgment. Employee training can be conducted in stand-alone programs that run for an hour or two, or may be included in new-hire programs, leadership development programs and general employee communications.

Ethics training should be considered as a matter of awakening employee's basic desire to do right. Enhancing individual abilities to recognize ethical situations will increase the frequency with which employees make moral considerations and use moral reasoning. Training should encourage improved moral sensitivity, improved moral decision-making, and the encouragement of virtues like integrity and courage as they might apply in a business
setting. Employees should be trained on how to analyze and judge a situation based upon relevant ethical principles, acting out of choice rather than of fear.

Training should not focus merely on memorization of

policies or laws; rather situations, role playing and personal stories should be included. Case situations of employees doing the right thing are especially important. The training should model the right behaviors in addition to calling attention to wrong behaviors. The social norms of the organization are perceived as a powerful influence on the ethicality of individuals, and exercises that include role playing and cases help clarify and emphasize social norms. Practical scenarios where employees can test their ethical knowledge are important aspects of training. Real-world examples and situations that are relevant to employee's jobs help drive home ethical concepts.

Some companies exempt high placed executives from legal and ethical training that is compulsory for other employees. This exemption should be avoided since it sends the signal that the company is delivering the training because it is required to, rather than the idea that it is a fundamental, respected corporate value.

Step 6: Provide Consistent Communication. A next step is to provide consistent and ongoing communications to all stakeholder groups – employees, customers, suppliers, investors, and the communities in which the organization has operations. Correspondence and reference materials should be developed and distributed to explain the program and its requirements for all. Some organizations have included handbooks, wall posters, signs, wallet cards, newsletters, and correspondence, annual reports, company magazines, and Websites as part of their multi-faceted communications efforts. Leaders should be cognizant that repetition is appropriate in any good communications campaign.

The most important component of any ethics program is senior management's continued public commitment to it. All the training in the world won't help if the company leaders don't live it. It needs to be regularly on the lips and pens of executives. The ethical message must be communicated in a variety of ways with routine frequency.

Step 7: Provide Confidential Resources. Most employees are reluctant to accuse fellow employees of ethical wrong-doing in an open forum. However, if given a private and confidential chance to convey information or ask questions about ethical practices they observe, they will readily do so. Consequently, organizations should provide confidential resources where employees can go with problems and concerns. These resources must be perceived to be reliable and trusted by employees.

Step 8: *Respond and Enforce Consistently, Promptly and Fairly.* The next step is to determine how ethical violations will be investigated, how violators will be sanctioned and how appeals will be conducted. The requirements are meaningless unless everyone understands what disciplinary mechanisms will be followed to enforce the requirements. Enforcement should involve punishment of the perpetrator. Termination and/or legal action may be deserved and help protect the organization from future ethical lapses.

Processes should work smoothly and efficiently, and roles and responsibilities should be clear and well documented. Once the organization has had a few years of consistent results, however, there is a tendency to let down the guard, a little. Managers may get lulled into a false sense of security, and adopt the attitude that the ethics compliance program is up and running and we need to devote our attention to other business challenges.
However, when the program gets ignored, ethical lapses can occur.

Step 9: Auditing, Monitoring and Reporting. In order to keep the organization from lapsing into a false sense of ethical security, the compliance program must be continually audited and monitored, and feedback must be provided   to   employees.   Unfortunately,   there   is   a temptation for individuals responsible for reporting to lose sight of the purpose of such activities, which is to identify any weaknesses to ethical conduct and correct them so that the organization improves over time. Human Resource professionals should track the number of employee grievance complaints, and evaluate employee responses to ethical attitude surveys. Another way to assess whether the ethics program is working is to include ethics questions on employee exit interviews.

Step 10: Make Continuous Improvements. The final step is to improve the organization's good ethical sensibilities. Continuous improvement should be based upon employee feedback and participation. Employees should be allowed to voice their opinions about the nature and effect of the code of conduct, the ethics officials, the delegation of authority, the communication and training programs, and the auditing activities.

When violations are detected, the organization must take steps to respond and to prevent further violations. Filling out forms, drafting carefully crafted policies, or producing lists of employees that have undergone training courses will not in and of itself improve the ethics of your company. A company should build a culture that encourages commitment to the law and to good ethical sense. Employees should know, for example, that no matter what the issue is and who is involved, deception, lying, fabricating records, or covering-up problems is
unacceptable. The standard of conduct is stated, applied, repeated, and understood by everyone in the organization regardless of job title or tenure.

While the headlines focus on the major indictable offenses like insider trading or corruption, most ethical errors aren't so obvious. There are smaller, often inconspicuous actions, such as personal use of company property, that foster an environment where ethical errors multiply. Continuously seeking out and correcting these
minor violations will help the organization avoid major lapses at some point in the future.

Ethical Leadership

In July 2006, a story was made public on how a Coca Cola Company employee and two accomplices attempted to sell trade secrets to rival Pepsi Cola Company. According to the story, one of the accomplices sent a letter to Pepsi claiming to be a high-placed Coca Cola official who was willing to sell confidential documents and new product samples for the right price. Pepsi exercised appropriate ethical leadership by promptly turning over the letter and envelope to Coca Cola's CEO, who contacted the FBI. An FBI undercover agent posed as a Pepsi executive and contacted the trio, negotiating a deal to purchase documents and a sample of product under laboratory development for $1.5 million. Surveillance photography caught the perpetrators on tape as they stole the documents and samples. All three were arrested the day the exchange was to be made.

Ethical leadership is not preaching, or the uttering of pieties, or the insistence on social conformity. Ethical leadership is responding correctly and decisively when an ethical dilemma emerges. When the trade secret offer letter arrived at Pepsi, at least one executive recognized that Pepsi's code of ethics required fair treatment of competitors, and this executive responded correctly by sending the offer letter to Coca Cola management. Pepsi spokesperson Dave DeCecco explained, "Competition can be fierce, but competition must also be fair and legal."

The ethical leader is characterized by high ideals and a strong sense of duty, by a strong drive for task completion, and for both vigor and persistence in pursuit of ethical goals. The ethical leader is self-confident and willing to accept consequences of decision and action; and has the capacity to structure social interaction to the purpose at hand. It takes true leadership to implement an ethics program in any organization.

Leadership is always associated with attainment of group

objectives. Leadership implies activity, movement and getting work done, and the leader is a person who occupies a position of responsibility in coordinating the activities of the members of the group in their task of attaining a common goal. The pattern of personal characteristics of the leader must bear some relevant relationship to the characteristics, activities and goals of the followers. If not, the followers will have difficulty identifying with the leader and difficulty in following his/her led.

Depending upon the situation, good ethical leaders engage in both participative and directive leadership. Directive leadership involves deciding and announcing the decision, selling the decision, and inviting questions. Participative leadership involves presenting tentative decisions subject to modifications, or presenting problems and asking for input, or defining limits and asking the group to make a choice. Subordinates vary in how much they like to participate in decisions. Participative leadership promotes acceptance of decisions and agreement to a greater extent than does directive leadership, but there is a time and place for both styles.

In our first chapter, we presented a framework for understanding ethical decision-making, and we'd like to return to it now. We've reprinted it on the following page as Figure 6-1.

As stated previously, the personal ethical standards of the leader has a very strong influence on the ethical behavior of others in the organization. Leaders need to have a well-formed conscience and self-confidence in expressing their views in order to inspire others to follow their ethical lead. As presented in chapter 2, leaders need an understanding of how the natural law – which includes precepts regarding honesty, fair treatment, self control, priorities, the value of human life, authority, and ownership – is supported by all of the major world religions. For the founders of our country and others informed by our Judeo-Christian heritage, the natural law is embodied in the second tablet of the Ten Commandments.

These values are consistent and unchanging aspects of the human condition, rising to the level of moral absolutes. If an organization, through its policies, products or programs, violates any natural law, an ethical leader should work to correct that violation immediately.

In addition, as presented in chapter 3, leaders need to understand the level of goal setting that is needed for the various decisions required by the organization. Decisions motivated by level 1 or level 2 goal setting, where the objective is to maximize the benefits of an individual or a small group, are usually inadequate for organizations. Leaders should challenge their executive team to strive for decisions at the fourth level of goal setting, and make sure that the third level is achieved in all situations at minimum.

The framework also suggests that the influences of stakeholders have a significant impact on the ethical behavior of the organization. As presented in chapter 4, leaders need to remember that the role of business is not to maximize profit, not to maximize the value to stakeholders, and not to achieve some moral minimum; rather it is to maximize business citizenship. That entails ordering business decisions so that the firm does good for society. Consequently, the ethical leader will consistently remind all stakeholders that the business citizenship responsibility of the firm is an important responsibility of the organization, and that benefits to each individual stakeholder group – employees, suppliers, shareholders, etc. – must be consistent with the overall business citizenship responsibility.

Figure 6-1

Framework for Understanding Ethical Decision-Making
Adapted from Ferrell, Fraedrich and Ferrell (2005)

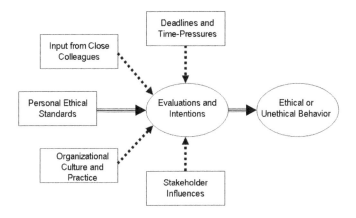

The framework also suggests that organization culture and practice has a huge impact on future ethical behavior, and consequently, a leader must work to establish an ethical culture among employees. As presented in chapters 5 and 6, the development of a respect for high legal and ethical standards requires an understanding of the law as a threshold and a commitment to engage in a whole series of actions that establishes ethical norms, trains employees to uphold them, assesses results, and continually works toward improving the ethicality of the entire organization. This requires outstanding ethical leadership at the top of the organization.

Despite the fact that Hewlett-Packard has a well-regarded ethics compliance program, such a program does not run itself. Effective leadership is still a necessary ingredient in making sure that the program continues to function over time. Unfortunately, even in the best of organizations, a lapse in leadership can have dire consequences. In October 2006, the Attorney General of California charged Hewlett-Packard CEO Patricia Dunn and other H-P executives with four felony counts of fraud and conspiracy. When these charges were announced, Patricia Dunn was forced to resign by the company's board of directors. (Later the California charges were dropped, but by then the public relations damage had been done and it was too late to save Dunn's job.)

What happened? The story began when confidential company plans were leaked to the financial press and Dunn initiated an investigation to determine the source of the leaks. During the conduct of the year-long investigation, private investigators employed by H-P apparently gathered some information unethically. They impersonated reporters and directors in an attempt to obtain phone records, and conducted a sting operation on an unsuspecting reporter in an attempt to get her to reveal her source. These actions certainly violated the H-P code of ethics, but apparently, no one required these outside investigators to abide by H-P's standards of conduct. When these facts came to light, the H-P board of directors demanded Dunn's resignation.

Patricia Dunn maintains that she was assured several times during the conduct of the investigation that the investigators were using legal means to obtain its information. But good ethical leadership should have required that someone in the H-P organization make sure that the investigation was being conducted according to H-P ethical standards. The person at the top of the organization bears the responsibility for oversight of the actions of lower-level operatives. Dunn's commitment to find the source of the leaks apparently overshadowed a responsible concern for how the investigation should be conducted.

Now It's Your Turn!

As we've seen, ethical mis-steps can lead to criminal convictions and imprisonment for executives, business failures, and significant loss of financial resources for shareholders. On the other hand, organizations with high ethical standards are more profitable and more successful over the long term than organizations without standards. Ethical compliance improves employee morale, and increases both recruitment and retention.

Organizations that establish a reputation of fairness and ethical behavior will attract outstanding candidates that will want to work for them; and attract other great companies that will want to do business with them. We've also seen that developing an organization that makes good ethical decisions requires leadership at the top. As a business leader, or as one aspiring to become one, the ball is now in your court. We've outlined what you must do to put the final pieces in place. Now is the time for action. Be an ethical leader now!

Summary

1. Winners can and do have high ethical standards.

2. An ethical organization does not happen by chance, and the adoption of codes of ethics, by itself, has not been an effective strategy. Instead, we recommend ten steps to develop a full and effective ethical compliance program.

3. The ten steps begin with organizational self-assessment, and continue with the creation of standards, organizational commitment, training, frequent communications, confidential resources, consistent response, implementation, auditing effectiveness, and ongoing program improvement.

4. Good ethical leadership requires responding correctly and decisively when an ethical dilemma emerges.

END NOTES

Foreword

AACSB International (2004), *Ethics Education in Business Schools: Report of the Ethics Education Task Force to AACSB International's Board of Directors*, St. Louis, MO: AASCB International.

Bowie, Norman (2001), "The Role of Business Ethics: Where Next? Is there a Role for Academics?" *Business Ethics: A European Review*, 10(4) October, 288-293.

Ferrell, OC, John Fraedrich and Linda Ferrell (2005), Business Ethics: Ethical Decision Making and Cases, 6th ed., Boston, MA: Houghton Mifflin Company.

Garten, Jeffrey E. (2005), "B-Schools: Only a C+ in Ethics," *BusinessWeek*, September 5, 110.

Hindo, Brian (2002), "Where Can Execs Learn Ethics?" *BusinessWeek Online*, 6/13/2002.

Verschoor, Curtis C. (2003), "Is Ethics Education of Future Business Leaders Adequate?" *Strategic Finance*, August, 22-23.

Williams, Scott D. and Todd Dewett (2005), "Yes, You Can Teach Business Ethics: A Review and Research Agenda," *Journal of Leadership and Organizational Studies*, 12(2).

Chapter 1

Callahan, David (2004), *The Cheating Culture: Why More Americans Are Doing Wrong to Get Ahead*, Harcourt, Inc.

Drumwright, Minette E. and Patrick E. Murphy (2004), "How Advertising Practitioners View Ethics: Moral Muteness, Moral Myopia and Moral Imagination," *Journal of Advertising*, 33(2), 7-24.

Emshwiller, John R., Gary McWilliams and Ann Davis (2006), "Symbol of an Era: Lay, Skilling Convicted of Conspiracy," *Wall Street Journal*, 267(123), A1, A9.

Ferrell, Fraedrich and Ferrell (2005) *Business Ethics: Ethical Decision Making and Cases*, 6th ed., Boston, MA: Houghton Mifflin Company.

Fleming, Jerry (2003), *Profit at Any Cost? Why Business Ethics Makes Sense*, Grand Rapids, MI: Baker Books.

Litzky, Barrie E., Kimberly A. Eddleston, and Deborah L. Kidder (2006), "The Good, the Bad, and the Misguided: How Managers inadvertently Encourage Deviant Behaviors,"   *Academy of Management Perspectives*, 20(1), 91-103.

Maxwell, John C. (2003), *There's No Such Thing as "Business" Ethics: There's Only One Rule For Making Decisions*, Warner Books.

Meisel, Steven and David S. Fearon (2006), "Choose the Future Wisely: Supporting Better Ethics Through Critical Thinking," *Journal of Management Education*, 30(1), 149-176.

Shih, Chia-Mei and Chin-Yuan Chen (2006), "The Effect of Organizational Ethical Culture on Marketing Managers' Role Stress and Ethical Behavioral Intentions," *Journal of American Academy of Business*, 8(1), 89-95.

Street, Marc and Vera Street (2006), "The Effects of Escalating Commitment on Ethical Decision-Making," *Journal of Business Ethics*, 64(4), 343-356.

Wall Street Journal (2006), "Symbol of an Era: Lay, Skilling Convicted of Conspiracy," Friday, May 26, page 1.

Chapter 2

Budzisvewski, J. (2002), "The Second Tablet Project," *First Things: A Monthly Journal of Religion & Public Life*, 124, 23-32.

Chonko, Lawrence B. (1995), *Ethical Decision Making in Marketing*, Sage Publications, Inc.

Flemming, Jerry (2003), *Profit at Any Cost? Why Business Ethics Makes Sense*, Grand Rapids, MI: Baker Books.

Gaustad, Edwin S. (1987), *Faith of Our Fathers: Religion and the New Nation*, Harper & Row.

Geroge, Robert P. (2001), *The Clash of Orthodoxies: Law, Religion and Morality in Crisis*, ISI Books.

Gomez-Lobo, Alfonso (2002), Morality and the Human Goods: An Introduction to Natural Law Ethics, Washington, DC: Georgetown University Press.

Lewis, Clive Staples (2001), *The Abolition of Man* or *Reflections on Education with Special Reference to the Teaching of English in the Upper Forms of Schools*, New York: HarperCollins Publishers, Inc.

Reck, Andrew J. (1989), "Natural Law and the Constitution," *Review of Metaphysics* 89(42), 483-511.

Shanahan, Timothy (1996), *Reason and Insight: Western and Eastern Perspectives on the Pursuit of Moral Wisdom*, Wadsworth.

Sokolowski, Robert (2006), "What Is Natural Law? Human Purposes and Natural Ends," chapter 14 in *Christian Faith and Human Understanding: Studies on the Eucharist, Trinity, and the Human Person*, Washington, DC: The Catholic University Press.

Wilken, Robert Louis (2003), "Keeping the Commandments," *First Things: A Monthly Journal* of *Religion & Public Life*, 137, 33-38.

Chapter 3

Anagnostopoulos, Georgios (1994), *Aristotle on the Goals and Exactness of Ethics*, Univ. of California Press.

Barclay, William (1993), *The Ten Commandments for Today*, Harper & Row Publishers.

Denise, T.C., Sheldon P. Peterfreund and Nicholas P. White (1996), *Great Traditions in Ethics*, Wadsworth Publishing Co.

Harrelson, Walter (1980), *The Ten Commandments and Human Rights*, Fortress Press.

Solomon, Robert C. (1993), *Ethics and Excellence, Cooperation and Integrity in Business*, Oxford University Press.

Spitzer, Robert J. (2000), *Healing the Culture*, Ignatius Press.

The Holy Bible, New International Version, Zondervan Publishing House, 1984.

Walterstorff, N. (1999), *National and Divine Law, Reclaiming the Tradition for Christian Ethics*, Eendmans Publishing Co.

Chapter 4

Business Ethics, The Magazine of Corporate Responsibility, (2006), Spring.

Enron – http://www.citizenworks.org/enron/enron_fact_sheet.pdf; http://www.globalethics.org/newsline/members/pastissue.tmpl?id=01210218015717&issueid=1/21/2002; http://news.bbc.co.uk/1/hi/business/1833221.stm

Tyco –http://www.securitiesfraudfyi.com/securities_fraud_faq.html

The Wall Street Journal, (2006), "Boeing to Settle Federal Probes for $615 Million," May 15.

WorldCom – http://www.aicpa.org/download/antifraud/121.ppt#21

Thorne McAlister, Debbie, O. C. Ferrell and Linda Ferrell (2005), *Business and Society: A Strategic Approach to Social Responsibility*, Houghton Mifflin.

Chapter 5

http://www.ceres.org/ceres/

Chapter 6

Anders, George and Alan Murray (2006), "Boardroom Duel: Behind H-P Chairman's Fall, Clash with a Powerful Director," *The Wall Street Journal*, Monday, October 9, p. 1.

Associated Press, "3 Stole Coke Secrets, Investigators Say," July 6, 2006.

Bass, Bernard M. (1981), *Stogdill's Handbook of Leadership: A Survey of Theory and Research*, New York: The Free Press.

Burns, James McGregor (1978), *Leadership*, Harper Collins Publishers, Inc.

Dessler, Gary (2005), "How to Fine-tune Your Company's Ethical Compass," *Supervision*, 15-17.

Dunn, Patricia (2006) "The H-P Investigation," *The Wall Street Journal*, Wednesday, October 11, p. A14.

Ferrell, Fraedrich and Ferrell (2005) *Business Ethics: Ethical Decision Making and Cases,* 6th ed., Boston, MA: Houghton Mifflin Company.

Frank, Robert H. (2005), *What Price the Moral High Ground?* Princeton University Press.

Kingsbury, Kathleen (2006), "You Can't Beat the Real Thing," *Time*, vol. 168, Issue 3, p. 9-10.

McKendall, Marie, Beverly DeMarr and Catherine Jones-Rik-
    kers (2002), "Ethical Compliance Programs and Corporate
    Illegality: Testing the Assumptions of the Corporate Sen-
    tencing Guidelines," *Journal of Business Ethics*, 37(4), 367-
    383.

Palmer, Daniel E. and Abe Zakhem (2001), "Bridging the Gap
    Between Theory and Practice Using the 1991 Federal Sen-
    tencing Guidelines as a Paradigm for Ethics training," *Jour-
    nal of Business Ethics*, 29, 77-84.

Reynolds, Scott J. and Norman E. Bowie (2004), "A Kantian
    Perspective on the Characteristics of Ethics Programs,"
    Business Ethics Quarterly, 14(2), 275-292.

Sele, Kathrin (2006), "Marketing Ethics in Emerging Markets
    – Coping with Ethical Dilemmas," *IIMB Management Review*
    (March).

Tyler, Kathryn (2005), "Do the Right Thing: Ethics Training
    Programs Help Employees Deal with Ethical Dilemmas,"
    HR Magazine, February, 99-102.

Wolken, Dan (2005), "Ward Best Known for Integrity," *The
    Colorado Springs Gazette*, June 22, 2005.

Made in the USA
Monee, IL
09 December 2020